T0321781

Decentralized Computing Using Blockchain Technologies and Smart Contracts:

Emerging Research and Opportunities

S. Asharaf
Indian Institute of Information Technology and Management, Kerala, India

S. Adarsh
Indian Institute of Information Technology and Management, Kerala, India

A volume in the
Advances in Information
Security, Privacy, and
Ethics (AISPE) Book Series

www.igi-global.com

Published in the United States of America by
IGI Global
Information Science Reference (an imprint of IGI Global)
701 E. Chocolate Avenue
Hershey PA 17033
Tel: 717-533-8845
Fax: 717-533-8661
E-mail: cust@igi-global.com
Web site: http://www.igi-global.com

Library of Congress Cataloging-in-Publication Data

Names: Asharaf, S., 1976- author. I Adarsh, S., 1988- author.
Title: Decentralized computing using blockchain technologies and smart
  contracts : emerging research and opportunities / by S. Asharaf and S.
  Adarsh.
Description: Hershey, PA : Information Science Reference, [2017] I Includes
  bibliographical references and index.
Identifiers: LCCN 2016056312I ISBN 9781522521938 (hardcover) I ISBN
  9781522521945 (ebook)
Subjects: LCSH: Database security. I Electronic data processing--Distributed
  processing. I Blockchains (Databases)
Classification: LCC QA76.9.D314 A94 2017 I DDC 005.8--dc23 LC record available at https://
lccn.loc.gov/2016056312

This book is published in the IGI Global book series Advances in Information Security, Privacy,
and Ethics (AISPE) (ISSN: 1948-9730; eISSN: 1948-9749)

British Cataloguing in Publication Data
A Cataloguing in Publication record for this book is available from the British Library.

Advances in
Information Security,
Privacy, and Ethics
(AISPE) Book Series

ISSN:1948-9730
EISSN:1948-9749

Editor-in-Chief: Manish Gupta, State University of New York, USA

MISSION

As digital technologies become more pervasive in everyday life and the Internet is utilized in ever increasing ways by both private and public entities, concern over digital threats becomes more prevalent.

The **Advances in Information Security, Privacy, & Ethics (AISPE) Book Series** provides cutting-edge research on the protection and misuse of information and technology across various industries and settings. Comprised of scholarly research on topics such as identity management, cryptography, system security, authentication, and data protection, this book series is ideal for reference by IT professionals, academicians, and upper-level students.

COVERAGE

- Privacy Issues of Social Networking
- Access Control
- Risk Management
- Security Classifications
- Privacy-Enhancing Technologies
- Global Privacy Concerns
- Cyberethics
- Technoethics
- Electronic Mail Security
- Computer ethics

IGI Global is currently accepting manuscripts for publication within this series. To submit a proposal for a volume in this series, please contact our Acquisition Editors at Acquisitions@igi-global.com or visit: http://www.igi-global.com/publish/.

Titles in this Series

For a list of additional titles in this series, please visit:
http://www.igi-global.com/book-series/advances-information-security-privacy-ethics/37157

For an enitre list of titles in this series, please visit:
http://www.igi-global.com/book-series/advances-information-security-privacy-ethics/37157

www.igi-global.com

701 East Chocolate Avenue, Hershey, PA 17033, USA
Tel: 717-533-8845 x100 • Fax: 717-533-8661
E-Mail: cust@igi-global.com • www.igi-global.com

Table of Contents

Preface

Blockchain technology is a decentralized, immutable data storage and management technology built by leveraging the idea of a distributed, consensus ledger. This technology was initially proposed by its illusive creator Satoshi Nakamoto as a global public ledger for storing the transaction history of the celebrated crypto currency called Bitcoin. In blockchains, the chronologically ordered transactional data are grouped into storage units called blocks. The blocks are then ordered sequentially and stored in a decentralized manner to form the public ledger called the blockchain. The inclusion of any transactional data in a blockchain requires an agreement, called consensus, between the various actors authenticated to confirm the said transaction. The actors may be humans or software agents empowered to validate the data included in the transaction. For each block, a publicly verifiable hash value is also computed, from the hash value of its predecessor block and the transactional data stored within the block. This publicly verifiable sequence of hash values associated with a blockchain easily enables the identification of any illegal modifications over the stored transactional data. Any tampering of the transactional data stored in the blockchain would demand the re-computation of the entire hash sequence, which is computationally very expensive. This makes the blockchains an immutable data store. The decentralized, distributed, consensus based public ledger approach with public verifiability using hash sequences makes Blockchains a trust free collaboration platform. It enables the people/agents with no confidence in each other to collaborate without the need of a trusted third party. In many a cases, the utility of a collaboration platform as explained above, would largely depend on the availability of any mechanism to specify and execute contractual agreements/obligations between collaborating entities. Such a mechanism called Smart Contract technology is also available with the blockchains. Smart contracts can enable actions/collaborations over the blockchain with the information stored in the blocks. The smart contracts technology also enables the creation and management of novel, virtual properties called smart properties.

Originally the blockchain technology was positioned as an enabling mechanism for crypto currencies. Later on its decentralized, distributed, immutable ledger capability attracted many e-Governance initiatives and this resulted its utilization in various Public Notary Services, Voting Systems, Citizen Identity Services, Passport Registration, and Migration Services. The positioning of blockchains as a trust free collaboration platform was identified as an opportunity in building the next generation Cyber Security systems and there are many ongoing research initiatives in this direction. The smart contract capability of blockchains over a distributed, decentralized data storage platform is perceived as a huge opportunity in implementing the revolutionary Decentralized Internet of Things paradigm. Many corporate entities and startups have already started investing in this compelling opportunity and a few innovative products and services have already surfaced in this arena. Financial products/services industry has also perceived blockchains with smart contracts as a huge opportunity to enable secure, trust free micro/ macro financial transactions with crypto/digital currencies instead of fiat currencies. Many mission critical tasks with heavy dependence on data validity and verifiability such as management of data in clinical trials is also being perceived as a potential opportunity for the application of blockchains with smart contracts. In a nutshell, blockchains with smart contracts is emerging as a high potential platform with secure, trust free, distributed and decentralized data storage enabling many novel technology business solutions.

Chapter 1
Overview of Computing Models

INTRODUCTION

From the early era of computing, centralization was the most preferred approach as it provided a sense of control and authority over the individuals and resources for the concerned. Historically, most of the organizations preferred centralization in their process flow to maintain the control within a limited group, and thus possibly retain the knowledge edge or monopoly in their respective business domains. *Centralized Computing* refers to the allocation of all computing/storage resources to a single unit which controls and facilitates all the computing/storage services for the organization. The focus of control in centralization is typically implemented with a server as the central node with appropriately networked low end computers as client terminals (Click et al., 2006). The centralized computing paradigm does the processing at the central server and all the client terminals can possibly act as connected thin clients. The thin client terminals will be having very limited or no computing capability. It is an attempt to improve efficiency by taking advantage of the potential economies of scale: improving the average; it may also improve reliability by minimizing the opportunities for failures/errors.

DOI: 10.4018/978-1-5225-2193-8.ch001

In earlier times, most of the organizations preferred centralized environment with mainframe computing and hence created large data centers within their control for physical and location consolidation. Hosting the data and services through a mainframe system ensured greater knowledge consolidation and protection for the organizations in their businesses (King, 1983). It also provided better staffing with talented brains focusing on the central servers for efficient and consistent performance. Centralization can create a simpler, easier-to-manage architecture which enable more standardization, control, and efficiency. But there should be well defined responsibilities and communication channel for all the nodes connected to central server for its proper working.

Centralized computing offers data integrity and avoids data redundancy which has predominant applications in most of the critical systems. It also helps to reduce the learning time for various processes as only a central server needs to be trained on the modifications. Centralization cuts the hardware and software licensing costs by the consolidation of requirements. The most prominent limitation of a centralized network is bandwidth. Since all data passes through a central node, that node is under a lot of pressure. Further, centralized systems entail a high initial cost disadvantage also (Corridori, 2012). They require costly infrastructure and a pool of experienced professionals for initial setup and maintenance. Moreover, failure to central server can make the entire system inoperable.

Figure 1. Centralized computing framework

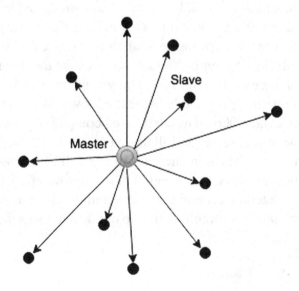

RISE OF DECENTRALIZED COMPUTING PLATFORMS

The idea of decentralization started way back from the era of human communication where human share information among each other to ensure that the knowledge does not get extinct by the loss of a single individual. Ancient tribes shared the vital information needed for their survival across generations in a decentralized manner and paved the way for the evolution of mankind. At the base level, decentralization is the simple process of taking information and distributing copies across the network so as to enhance security, redundancy, trust, accessibility, and congruence. *Decentralized* computing distributes computing capabilities to many nodes spread across the network. The network consists of a collection of autonomous computers that may be geographically separated, but can communicate with each other across a network to provide a common, agreed upon service (Suryanarayana, 2006). The concept of decentralization kick-started in the computing paradigm after realizing its potential in accelerating the decision-making processes for faster and efficient problem solving in diverse business domains. In a generic sense, the decentralization takes over the control from the governments and central entities to the peer-to-peer network with immutable mathematical logic *that* provides better security, efficiency and resilience with reduced timeframe and overheads.

A typical example of the decentralization technology is the Bittorrent protocol, the first file-sharing application over a distributed and decentralized peer-to-peer network (Johnsen et al., 2005). It gained considerable popularity as the files can be shared/uploaded/downloaded easily among peer entities even on a network with minimal bandwidth. The Bittorrent protocol breaks a single file into smaller pieces and distributes it to all the users across the network who wants to download that file. The users can simultaneously download the file pieces from other users who have already downloaded its copy, making the download even faster. This mutual sharing of smaller file pieces across the peer-to-peer network make the Bittorrent protocol efficient for sharing large files to multiple users more faster and efficient. Most of the file sharing applications now tends to follow the decentralized architecture of Bittorrent protocol to tackle the issue of low network bandwidth (Toole et al., 2006).

Decentralized computing enjoys the freedom of diverse computer architectures, terminal types and organizational procedures linked together to adapt to the ever-growing needs of different environments. This allows flexibility in improving the functionalities and capacity of the system through which it explores wider business potentials effectively. With the power of modularity, the decentralized computing improves the availability and manageability of resources across various geographical sites which improve the response-time to service requests on the system (Beck, 2010). Modularity also ensures non-disruptive modifications to system since updating one service will not affect another. It also supports faster and cost-efficient network growth as new nodes can be added easily. Further, decentralized computing can effectively function on a low bandwidth network as opposed to a centralized computing which demand huge bandwidth at the server side. This is primarily because the service requests get distributed across the different sites in the decentralized computing infrastructure and thus avoid the heavy network load on any particular location.

Generally, the decentralized platforms will have a message protocol that interlinks all the nodes across the peer-to-peer network to support modularity and ensure efficient communication. This can also improve the speed and flexibility with increase in the local control and execution of a service. Since

Figure 2. Decentralized computing

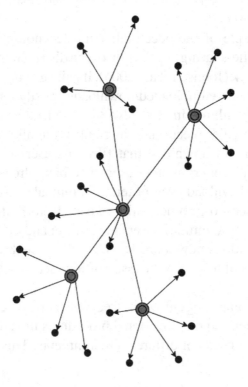

there is no single central authority that makes decisions on behalf of all the stakeholders, each stakeholder or peer makes local autonomous processing and provides results towards its individual goals which may possibly contradict with those of other peers. This is a potential challenge of decentralization, which we will discuss in the coming chapters. The peers in the network can directly interact with each other and share data or provide computing capabilities and services to other peers. Eventually, the effectiveness of decentralization depends on the coordination and cooperation among the peer nodes of the network.

Decentralized computing provides the great advantage of low down-time and fault tolerance as the failure of certain nodes will not paralyze the entire network. It allows efficient overhauling of various network components at lower cost and time. Decentralization can also remove and replace the monolithic central servers and helps in easier and faster updating of hardware and software systems.

Decentralized computing allows specialization, which helps the businesses to offer more refined services to the clients. Specialization improves the processing speed as the computations will be more focused towards catering the diverse needs of the clients. Decentralization gives individual business units autonomy over their own resources without any major considerations over other resources and provides increased attention to personal/local preferences in the overall system. The decentralized platforms provide organizational flexibility, scalability and responsiveness through increased autonomy. In the context of Blockchain technology, a decentralized computing platform can be viewed as formed of three major components -*a decentralized networking component* (mesh networks), *a decentralized transactions component (the* blockchain technology *)* and a *decentralized decision making component* (autonomous agents) (Wall Street Journal, 2014). Our interest in this book is confined largely with the second part – the blockchain technology.

Blockchain is simply a huge distributed public ledger shared amongst all the participating nodes in the network, and keeps an immutable record of every single successful transaction (Crosby et al., 2016). With the evolution of self-executing contracts called smart contracts, the terms of deed and agreements can be embedded over the blockchains. These public ledgers powered by smart contracts makes the performance of any transactions (including payments), identity verifications, trust and reputation management etc. programmable and quantifiable, which turns out to be a mandatory requirement in a wide array of business scenarios. We will explore further on blockchains and the smart contracts in the coming chapters.

CHALLENGES IN DECENTRALIZATION

In the earlier days, there was a constant fear among the nodes of a decentralized environment that the information may fall into the hands of malicious individuals. Thus well defined security and privacy norms were important to ensure the balance among centralized and decentralized structures for information sharing. To solve the problem of privacy, cryptographic hashing approaches were introduced in the decentralized computing. The modern cryptographic hashing algorithms are highly efficient in ensuring privacy and thus eliminate the possibility of data leakage during an attack. This is achieved by the simple logic that the data cannot be re-created back from the hash values. Other major challenges encountered with decentralized computing were the higher cost for management of infrastructure, the need for the aggregation of historical information, and the difficulty and cost involved in the rollout of any new enhancements (The Net Galaxy, 2016). Some of the other major challenges of a decentralized platform are:

- **Missing Universal Control:** It would be difficult to know the role and services of every node in the decentralized network. Contradictory actions may be taken by different peers over a common scenario due to the lack of a universal control. Thus there can be discrepancies over services provided by different nodes in the environment. In this context, the consensus strategies are evolving as a possible solution to resolve this issue (The Net Galaxy, 2016).
- **Attacker Collusion:** The attackers may join together to misuse the entire system. This group may decide to collude in order to inflate their own trust values and deflate trust values for peers that are not in the collective.
- **Data Fudging:** The attackers will initiate fraudulent activities to perform data fudging so that genuine users may get cheated. This will eventually reduce the trust on the system and the services may get affected badly.
- **Denial of Service:** This is one of the most important types of attack in any decentralized environment. These types of attacks disable the regular functionalities offered by the system or interrupt the normal operations. Spamming and flooding of genuine users with unwanted messages may also happen in this context (The Net Galaxy, 2016).

- **Forgery:** Attackers will try to impersonate their identities and can act as legitimate users. These attackers will mimic the trust relationship with legitimate users.
- **Foreign Entities:** During the start of the system the peers will not know each other and every node will be foreign to the system. This opportunity can be leveraged during this period for attacking the system.

Since the inception of the decentralization paradigm, the modern computing world was in search for the potential solutions to solve the above said challenges. With the revolutionary concepts of Blockchain Technology unleashed by Nakamoto, most of these challenges were addressed easily and efficiently. This resulted in the adoption of Blockchain technology as the most preferred option in building decentralized platforms for solving problems in a diverse set of application domains.

FUTURE OF DECENTRALIZED COMPUTING

Even though the Internet was designed in a distributed fashion, today's web is mostly centralized, with the dominance of internet giants like Microsoft, Google, Apple, Twitter etc. Present day internet is too fragile as it relies mostly on centralized paradigm, with servers that can be added or removed. If any server goes down for some reason or is removed, all the web pages stored on that server disappear.

In order to overcome this trouble of centralization and to enjoy the freedom of access and expansion capabilities most of the governmental and non-governmental organizations of the current era are gearing up for adopting the decentralization paradigm. In the competitive internet businesses, the demand for zero downtime is an inevitable component but a nightmare in most centralized platforms. With the adoption of decentralization, the zero down time will become a norm rather than a pressing need as in the age old centralized systems. For survival in the fast paced and connected modern world, businesses need expansion in full throttle to offer competitive but cost effective operations/services in different geographical locations. In this context, the decentralized computing cuts down the cost of dedicated servers and improves efficiency with localized operations which is extremely important for cost effective and rapid expansion. Further, decentralization can also offer fine grained/localized flexibility and better resilience to failures as compared to any centrally governed, corporate entities.

The smart contracts are another opportunity in decentralized platforms using blockchains. The smart contracts introduce programmability with better privacy and security when building services/applications in the decentralized environment. The decentralized platforms will work only on the basis of smart contracts and these contractual statements can never be tampered or altered by any individual in the network.

The Internet of Things, which was primarily focused on centralized computing, is shifting gears to decentralized platforms for wider reach and for accommodating larger array of devices. Any realistic centralized implementation of IoT accommodating all sorts of things (devices) in context will definitely incur a high cost on the centralized computing infrastructure. Further, it may not be scalable also. In this context, the decentralized peer-to-peer networks will be a boon to the ever-growing IoT, as more and more devices exploring various tracks of human life are being developed (Pureswaran et al., 2015). Decentralized platforms can work even in low bandwidth connections which makes it easier to establish connections across the network. With the advent of intelligent systems and self-learning machines, every device require freedom of operation and performs individual decision making even if committed to a network, which can be realized only through decentralization.

REFERENCES

Beck, M. (2010). *Centralized versus Decentralized Information Systems in Organizations.* Emporia State University.

Click, R., Shutzberg, L., & Buren, M. V. (2006). *Centralized vs. Distributed Computing: How to Decide.* ExecBlueprints.

Corridori, A. F. (2012). *What is Centralized Computing.* Retrieved July 5, 2016 from http://idcp.marist.edu/enterprisesystemseducation/zinsights/ECI%20No.%202%20Cent%20Comp%20v2c.pdf

Crosby, M., Pattanayak, P., Verma, S., & Kalyanaraman, V. (2016). Blockchain technology: Beyond bitcoin. *Applied Innovation*, (2), 6-10.

Johnsen, J. A., Karlsen, L. E., & Birkeland, S. S. (2005). *Peer-to-peer networking with BitTorrent.* Department of Telematics, NTNU.

King, J. L. (1983). Centralized versus decentralized computing: Organizational considerations and management options. *ACM Computing Surveys*, *15*(4), 319–349. doi:10.1145/289.290

MSG. (2016). *Centralization and Decentralization*. Retrieved from http://www.managementstudyguide.com/centralization_decentralization.htm

Pureswaran, V., Panikkar, S., Nair, S., & Brody, P. (2015). *Empowering the edge: Practical insights on a decentralized Internet of Things*. IBM Institute for Business Value.

Suryanarayana, G. (2006). *Decentralization: PACE Project*. Retrieved from http://isr.uci.edu/projects/pace/decentralization.html

The Next Galaxy. (2016). *The Advantages and Disadvantages of Decentralization*. Retrieved from http://thenextgalaxy.com/the-advantages-and-disadvantages-of-decentralization/

Toole, R., & Vokkarane, V. (2006). *Bittorrent architecture and protocol*. University of Massachusetts Dartmouth.

Wall Street Journal. (2014). *The Imminent Decentralized Computing Revolution*. Retrieved from http://blogs.wsj.com/accelerators/2014/10/10/weekend-read-the-imminent-decentralized-computing-revolution/

Chapter 2
Introduction to Blockchain Technology

INTRODUCTION

Blockchain technology is a decentralized data storage technology originally proposed by the illusive creator Satoshi Nakamoto in 2008 as the back-end for the celebrated crypto-currency Bitcoin (Nakamoto, 2008). (Later on, an Australian Computer Scientist, Craig Wright claims himself as Satoshi Nakamoto in his blog, the truth is yet to be proved). During the initial days, the world was concerned only about the currency, Bitcoin and it's mining while the underlying technology was neglected. The initial releases of Blockchain, known as Blockchain 1.0 focused mainly on crypto-currencies and micro-payments and provided less scope for programming the chain of business applications. The common man was unaware of the potential and possibilities of blockchain technology as the Bitcoin and its market cap overshadowed the underlying technology. Later on, with the release of Blockchain 2.0, the focus got shifted from currencies to the value based services and applications. Blockchain 2.0 enables the creation of programmable, scalable, distributed, trust infrastructure which facilitates wide variety of services including smart contracts, public ledger systems, Dapps (decentralized applications), DAOs (decentralized autonomous organizations), and DACs (decentralized

DOI: 10.4018/978-1-5225-2193-8.ch002

autonomous corporations). Moreover, with the advent of Blockchain 2.0, this technology came into the limelight as a potential solution for various business opportunities and the programmable smart contracts created a new dimension for self-executing applications. Blockchain technology can play a significant role in transfer of value-based digital assets across the network in a faster and cheaper manner. By leveraging the potential of distributed public ledger system, blockchain technology found its application in government institutions like public notary systems, land registrations, citizen identification services, marriage certificates, voting systems etc. Eventually, people started placing the blockchain as a disruptive technology that could possibly find "The Best Solution" for several real-world problems (Crosby et al.,2016).

Inside Blockchains

As the word sounds, Blockchain is actually a chain of blocks connected sequentially. In blockchains, the chronologically ordered data points are grouped into individual storage units called blocks. These blocks are then ordered sequentially and stored in a decentralized manner across all the participating nodes to form the blockchain. Each time a block gets completed, a new block is generated. Blockchain technology was highly cherished for having the legendary concept of "Immutable data store" which was a dream in the computing world for many decades. Hashing technique plays a vital role in creating immutable data stores. For imparting immutability to the blockchains, a hash value is computed and locally stored inside each block using its content and the hash value of its immediate predecessor. The hash function is designed in such a way that it is very complex to compute, but easy to verify. This sequence of hash functions for the chronologically ordered blocks thus forms a publicly available, easy to verify mechanism for protecting the contents of the blockchains. Due to the chronological dependency on the previous block, the hash value stored at each node cannot be tampered in isolation. The publicly verifiable sequence of hash functions associated with the blockchain makes any illegal modification easily identifiable. Also, any such tampering would demand the re-computation of the entire hash chain, which is computationally very expensive and this makes the blockchain an "immutable data store". Simply, the Blockchain technology can be viewed as an innovative approach of creating a secure public ledger that leverages the potential of peer-to-peer networks, cryptographic hashing and distributed consensus approach over a complex mathematical puzzle (Nakamoto, 2008).

Figure 1. A simple blockchain model

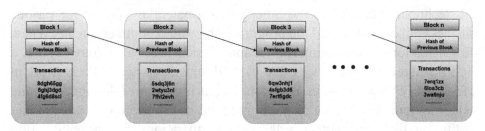

Once a block is added to the distributed public ledger, it's extremely difficult to modify or remove it. Whenever a node wants to add contents to the chain, every node in the blockchain network runs the consensus algorithm to evaluate and checks the proposed transaction and the node history. The node can be either an individual or a group of miners or a machine powered with smart contract. If a majority of nodes agrees on the validity of transaction, then it will be approved and will be added to the new block in the chain. Usually, the criteria for majority and number of confirmations required will be embedded into the first block (genesis block) of the blockchain using smart contracts. Some of the attractive features, for which the blockchains were highly praised in the computing world, are:

- Every node in the blockchain network can converge on a consensus strategy of the latest version of distributed public ledger, even with dishonest and anonymous nodes to ensure that no attack takes place on the blockchain.
- Every valid node participating in the blockchain network has the ability to determine the validity of a transaction and gains reward on successful completion of consensus.
- Blockchains facilitates efficient transaction among unknown entities without the help of trusted intermediaries'. The blockchain network can also eliminate the double-spent problem and conflicting transactions in the network.
- Blockchain network charges extremely high cost to modify or rewrite a transaction which makes the transactions.

Possibility of Attack on Blockchains

Attacking a Blockchain will be one of the most exciting experiments ever conducted on the decentralized environment. Many enthusiasts are formulating various ways to crack the rock-solid framework of blockchains. The skeleton of blockchain exists around a large number of nodes connected to form a distributed network. Every single node in the network have a copy of the entire blockchain which makes the attacking/hacking extremely difficult but easier to detect and eliminate. Suppose an attacker tries to alter the transactions in an intermediate block, then he have to make the changes in that block and redo all the succeeding blocks till the present block within a short time in which every valid nodes works on the consensus to create the present block. This would be a highly expensive process in terms of computational power spent within the time span of creation of a new block. Even if a hacker succeeds in any attempt with some extreme computing capability, the change will be reflected to only one node and blockchain content at all the other nodes will not be affected. The suspect could be easily caught and the chain can be recovered with zero down-time and thus completely eliminates the need for an intermediary or trusted-third party to find the culprits. Each node in the blockchain helps in developing a trust-free distributed environment through the peer-to-peer consensus network. This property of nodes improves the reliability of blockchain network to make it suitable for data management.

With these cutting-edge features, Blockchain technology promises to ensure tamper-proof, censorship-resistant, immutable, trust-free and non-intermediated distributed digital platforms, open for all to freely innovate and to transact on which helps in creating value across the platforms for various domains. By removing the intermediary data synchronization and concurrency control, it will also help to meet industry-level requirements by radically lowering the "cost of trust and time". Blockchains powered with smart contracts offer significantly higher returns for every penny spent through it than the traditional methods. Because, every transaction can happen only with the compliance of contractual agreement and every violations are truncated. In essence, the investment over every transaction gets rewarded in a right manner and the wastages will be minimized drastically.

History of Blockchains

The concept of digital currency through a decentralized platform without the control of any governmental body has been around for decades. People started thinking about digital currencies as the fiat currencies faced many setbacks and got devalued due to economic crisis at various occasions. Also, many people lost trust on fiat currencies as its value highly depend on political pressure and insecurities. Thus the world stared thinking of a global currency that could be termed as a secure investment can exist beyond barriers of governments for any transaction. In 1983, David Chaum introduced a digital signature known as blind signature in which the content of the message is blinded before it is signed. During the early 80s anonymous e-cash protocols were following this cryptographic approach commonly called Chaumian Blinding (Chaum, 1984). This technique provided high degrees of privacy to the digital currencies, but this approach was largely dependent on the centralized control which regulates the operations. The centralized approach was considered as a major flaw a people lost trust on these systems for digital transfers. Later, in 1998, Wei Dai came up with the concept of b-money which introduced the idea of creating money through solving computational puzzles as well as decentralized consensus. But he failed to explain the consensus approach to level of acceptance to technocrats and common people. In 2005, Hal Finney introduced a concept of "reusable proofs of work", which combined the ideas from Wei Dai's b-money together with Adam Back's Hashcash puzzles to create a concept for a cryptocurrency, but once again fell short of the ideal by relying on trusted computing as a backend. In 2009, decentralized cryptocurrency named Bitcoin was introduced by an illusive creator Satoshi Nakamoto, utilizing the concept of Public key cryptography and Proof of work based consensus which efficiently demonstrated a stand-alone currency in a decentralized world.

Nakamoto's Public Ledger for Bitcoin

Satoshi Nakamoto proposed an electronic payment system based on cryptographic proof instead of the regular trust-based ones, which allows any two concerned parties to make transactions directly with each other without the need for a trusted third party. Nakamoto, which might be the pseudonym for the creator of Bitcoin published the white paper on crypto-currency *"Bitcoin: A Peer-to-Peer Electronic Cash System"* on October 31, 2008 through metzdowd.com. All the transactions are computationally impractical to reverse which would protect the involved parties from attackers. Bitcoin is a well-known crypto-currency which came into existence by January 2009 with the development of Bitcoin network. Earlier, on August 2008 Neal Kin, Vladimir Oksman, and Charles Bry filed an application for an encryption patent, but they denied any connection with Nakamoto. Bitcoin.org domain was registered on anonymousspeech.com website on August 15, 2008 well before publishing the original whitepaper on Bitcoin. On November 09, 2008 Bitcoin Project was registered on SourceForge.net, which is a community collaboration website aimed at development and distribution of open source software (Crosby et al., 2016).

The first block of bitcoin (genesis block) was mined on January 3, 2009 at 18:15:05 GMT which paved way for the distribution of first decentralized digital currency in the world. As the genesis block was mined, the first version of Bitcoin was released on January 9, 2009 that would create a total of 21 million Bitcoins through the year 2040. Bitcoins can be freely mined by anyone on the world by installing the bitcoin miner software. On January 12, 2009, Nakamoto made the first-ever Bitcoin currency transaction with Hal Finney, a crypto-currency activist. The exchange rates for bitcoin was established by New Liberty Standards at a value US\$1=1309.03BTC on October 5, 2009. Later on the complexity of mining Bitcoins was increased as more and more coin gets mined. It's estimated that by January 2011, 25 percent of total bitcoins were mined and by March 2011 bitcoin reaches parity with US dollars. The users of bitcoins were termed as "Miners" as they use the Bitcoin Miner software to mine the digital currency. These miners create new blocks which contains details regarding the bitcoin transactions. An important scalability feature of Bitcoin is that the block is stored in a multi-level data structure. The "hash" of a block is actually only the hash of the block header, a roughly 200-byte piece of data that contains the timestamp, nonce, previous block hash and the root hash of a data structure called the Merkle tree storing all transactions in the block. The Merkle tree protocol is arguably essential to long-term sustainability. According to sources, a "full node" in the Bitcoin network, the one that stores and processes the entirety of every block, takes up about 15 GB of disk space in the Bitcoin network as of April 2014, and is growing by over a gigabyte per month.

The most interesting part of Bitcoin is the real–time public ledger running at backend which stores every transaction that had ever occurred. Bitcoin used the blockchain technology as its peer-to-peer distributed transaction ledger which is anonymous and permission-less. More and more users were attracted towards the Bitcoin network by knowing about the tamper-free public ledger using cryptographic hashing which was controlled by the underlying block-chain technology. Even without the trusted intermediary financial institutions and global banks, people found out that blockchain technology was much secure and cheaper than the fiat currency transactions. The public ledger also avoided the chances of fraud and double-spend problem in transactions. The public ledger support made the transactions more transparent and ubiquitous which was a boon for both lump sum and micro payments. This distributed ledgers also avoided the over-burden of auditing and inspection as they are self-audited by the bitcoin miners which again saved time and cost for third party auditing and other related accounting activities. Nakamoto's whitepaper unveiled two radical concepts, a decentralized peer-to-peer digital currency and the concept of proof-of-work based blockchain technology that works on public consensus strategy which created possibilities for breathtaking revolutions in the digital world. These awesome findings are going to be the greatest technology disruptions of the twenty first century (Bitcoin Foundation Wiki, 2016).

Bitcoin addresses are directly derived from public keys generated by elliptic-curve DSA, and transactions are authenticated using digital signatures. The public keys and signatures are published as part of the publicly available and auditable blockchain to prevent double-spending. Each transaction was recorded on the blockchain ledger, the newest block tied to the ones before it using a digital signature. To ensure trust in the ledger, participants on the network ran complicated algorithms to verify those digital signatures and add transactions to the blockchain. Bitcoin makes use of two hashing functions, SHA-256 and RIPEMD-160, but it also uses Elliptic Curve DSA on the curve secp256k1 to perform signatures (Nakamoto, 2008).

Nakamoto's incentive-based mining attracted many people to Bitcoin mining software as the reward goes to the first miner who can present a proof-of-work for a valid block. That means, with a hash value less than the current limit for a new block, which is accepted and agreed by the majority of other miners as being legitimate and consistent with the mining protocols that govern transactions. These mining rewards were issued in terms of Bit-coins which will eventually promote more transactions using Bitcoins and improve its market cap. Once a valid block has been added to the chain, the other miners should accept it, give up their own effort, and start work on the following block. The rising market value of Bitcoins accelerated the competition among miners to mine more and more coins by performing intense mining. Eventually, hash limit is continually being adjusted downwards, as it's important that the amount of work remains significant even as the mining hardware gets faster.

CREATION OF IMMUTABLE BLOCKS

The digital world is in constant race to develop solutions to tackle data fudging, illicit modifications and tampering by known and unknown entities. Huge amount of money are being paid to third-party organizations to ensure security, privacy and immutability of data. Even though it drains out majority of the working capital of most of the businesses, many companies are ready to pay these huge amounts for the cause of security as they are left with no other options. Rather, most of the businesses need to ensure immutability to showcase their credibility. "Immutability" refers to the property of an object whose state cannot be changed once it is created. As we discussed earlier, Blockchain is one of the most promising technologies that can inherently provide the vital property of "immutability" through the tamper-proof blocks being created in the chain. By unleashing the variety of flavors such as cryptographic hashing, mining etc. to affirm immutability, blockchains open up immense potential to tackle the conventional trust-related problems in a simpler and efficient manner. Moreover, it also disrupts the tiresome auditing and authentication processes with the freedom of decentralized immutable data stores and serves to generate good profit for the businesses.

Immutability is highly appreciable in ensuring data security as the data stored in a block of the blockchain persists forever. The immutable data ensures easier auditing and reliability to the data stored in the blocks. Excitingly, even the owners or nodes of the network cannot alter the contents of blocks as any modification to the blocks will be highly expensive and requires significant computational power. Each block in a blockchain is a computer code containing some form of information, such as a contract, certificate of authentication or data. The transaction data are permanently recorded in files called blocks. These blocks help in chronological ordering of data over a network of trust-free nodes (Swan, 2015).

Building a Block

Building a block is the primary task for every node in the blockchain network as they get rewarded for this process. In the blockchain network, every transaction generated by a node is digitally signed with the hash of previous transaction and the public key of next node, who receives the transaction in order to make sure that they are tamper-proof. These transactions are broadcasted to the entire blockchain network. Each node in the blockchain network will collect the transaction into their block and works on finding the proof-of-work (POW) for its block. Proof-of work is simply a slice of data generated as a computational solution which is difficult to produce, but easier to verify. After finding the proof-of-work for a block, the node will broadcast it around the network. Every node in the network has to accept the block by working on creating the next block in the chain, using the hash of the accepted block as the previous hash. This process of adding transaction records into the blockchain's public ledger is known as *mining*. Also the participating nodes in the blockchain network who works on the concept of proof-of-work to create blocks are known as *miners*.

Without the miners, the blockchain network may collapse and will lose its value. All the transactions made are authorized by miners, which makes the transactions immutable and prevent it from the threat of hacking. With more miners on the network, it is less likely for any one individual miner to monopolize the ability to choose transaction order. Mining involves an attempt to find a numerical value called "nonce" which when combined with other open transactions generates a hash which satisfies certain level of "difficulty". The level of difficulty increases the computational cost and time making the blockchain tamper-proof. Every block has a header that stores the metadata which includes block reference number, address of previous block and timestamp of block creation (Lewis, 2015)

Miners maintain a copy of the entire blockchain and monitor the blockchain network for the newly announced transactions. For obtaining rewards, miners compete with each other to complete the work, which is to "wrap-up" the current block such that it is being accepted by other nodes in the network. These wrapped up block that has to be accepted includes a solution of Proof of work computation known as "hash". The more computing power a miner possess, the higher their "hash-rate" and the greater their odds of solving the current block. The first miner to solve the block containing the committed transactions announces the newly-solved block to the blockchain network. If all the other participating nodes agree that the block is valid, the new block is added to the blockchain and the entire process begins afresh. Once added to the blockchain the transaction state changes from "pending" to "confirmed". Generally, the Bitcoin blockchain requires six confirmations to validate a transaction for ruling out any chances of illegal operation. Bitcoin blockchain also produced blocks at an interval of ten minutes with the maximum waiting time being one hour.

Shaping the Immutable Data Store

During the initial period, Bitcoin did not gained much acceptance as people were in doubt about the credibility and market value of a cryptocurrency being generated by software. Later on, people started pondering on the hidden treasure of Nakamoto's concept and explored more about blockchains. The blockchain technology provides an immutable data store which stores the data permanently in its blocks. The versatile property of immutability nurtures in the blocks by the huge expense of computational power to be spend by the participating nodes for modifying a stored transaction. Also the consensus approach ensures that every participating node in the blockchain have to agree upon a common strategy for editing a transactions. This makes it practically impossible for modifying or editing the data in the blocks unless every node agrees over the consensus to spent their computational power to do the same. The Bitcoin blockchain was just used for storing the bitcoin transactions but this can be extended to greater potential to other domains as an immutable data store. With the ownership and provenance of a transaction recorded in the blockchain at the beginning of a transaction and verified across the mining process, agreement among all individuals involved in a transaction is guaranteed.

As mentioned earlier, the chronological order of transactions are maintained when the transactions are added to the blocks. The blockchains generally form an append-only data store, which means that data can be only added to the chain, but cannot be taken way. Blockchain data storage could be disruptive. Current cloud storage services are centralized — thus users must place trust in a single storage provider. With the Blockchain, this can become decentralized and has immense potential for various business domains. For instance, Storj is beta-testing cloud storage using a Blockchain-powered network to improve security and decrease dependency. By the research conducted by Storj Labs, world spends over $22 billion for cloud storage yearly. Out of this huge amount 31% accounts for privacy concerns, 34% for cost concerns and 32% for security concerns. According to Shawn Wilkinson (Storj Labs), by utilizing the excess hard drive space, users could store the traditional cloud 300 times over. This could open a revenue stream for average users, while significantly reducing the cost to store data for companies and personal users.

Longest Valid Chain

Suppose there are two miners X and Y located at geographically distant locations over the blockchain network that solves the present block to be added roughly at the same time. X propagates the block BX_1 and Y propagates the block BY_1 over the network resulting in two competing versions of blocks over the network. So, who is the winner? The answer is quite simple. The longest valid chain among the two becomes the legitimate version. Suppose the next miner solves the proof of work and add block to the chain of X creating BX_2. If BX_2 propagates across the network and confirms before BY_2 is found then the chain of X will be declared as winner. Y is defeated by X in the race and Y loses the mining rewards and its chain will be invalid.

Mining Difficulty

This concept was introduced first in Bitcoin Blockchain to set a control over the coins being mined and to ensure that the coins do not get exhausted. *It is simply* an algorithm to regulate issuing of coins, which adjusts the difficulty of the Proof of Work problem in accordance with how quickly blocks are solved within a certain timeframe. Difficulty rises and falls with deployed hashing power to keep the average time between blocks to around 10 minutes.

Need of Proof of Work (POW)

The term proof-of-work (POW) was first formally defined by Markus Jakobsson and Ari Juels in 1999. POW can be coined as a computational puzzle which could solved only by spending certain amount of CPU power of the user and cannot be attempted manually. This potential of POW was utilized by the blockchain technology to establish an asymmetrical computation paradigm such that the computation must be challenging (but feasible) on the requester side but easy to verify for the service provider (Jakobsson et al., 1999). Nakamoto utilized the concept of POW to solve the Double-Spend problem and to create the distributed trust-free consensus platform. For realizing this distributed consensus mechanism, Nakamoto had extended the potential of original POW algorithm with cryptographic signatures, merkle chains, and peer-to-peer networks (Price, 2016).

The premier blockchain application, Bitcoin used a POW system similar to Adam Back's Hashcash mechanism and was commonly known as Bitcoin mining (Back, 2002). The Bitcoin miners require computers with very high computational power like GPU machines to compete with fellow nodes to solve POW in lesser time to earn Bitcoins. The POW involves finding a nonce (integer) which when hashed together with the block header data will give an output with given number of leading zero's which depend on the current mining difficulty. Another modification of POW is Proof-of-Stake (POS). In POS, the decision is taken on the basis of the percentage of ownership of each stakeholder in the application rather than the computational power. POS is generally used in scenarios where nodes in the blockchain have varying roles and privileges over the transactions happening in the network. POS ensures a kind of authority to every node based on its relevance in specific area of application. Depending on the situations, both POW and POS can be used simultaneously in a blockchain network.

As we are now familiar with the basic concepts involved in building a block, lets explore the structure of a block in detail.

Since each block references the previous one with its hash, every block is guaranteed to come after the previous block chronologically from the genesis block (first block). Otherwise the previous block's hash would not be known. Each block is also computationally impractical to modify once it has been in the chain for a while because every block after it would also have to be regenerated which makes every transaction unique and removes duplicates. In order to reduce the space utilization, every hashed transaction are paired and hashed again iteratively like in merkle tree until a single hash value remains. This single hash value will be the merkle root which is stored in the block header. A Merkle tree is a type of binary tree, composed of a set of nodes with a large number of leaf nodes at the bottom of the tree containing the underlying data, a set of intermediate nodes where each node is the hash of its two children, and finally a single root node, also formed from the hash of its two children, representing the "top" of the tree. The purpose of the Merkle tree is to allow the data in a block to be delivered piecemeal: a node can download only the header of a block from one source, the small part of the tree relevant to them from another source, and still be assured that all of the data is correct. Nakamoto explains the reason why this works is

Figure 2. Simplified structure of a block

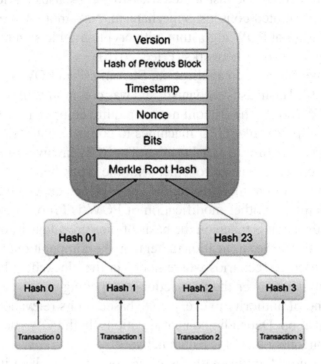

that hashes propagate upward: if a malicious user attempts to swap in a fake transaction into the bottom of a Merkle tree, this change will cause a change in the node above, and then a change in the node above that, finally changing the root of the tree and therefore the hash of the block, causing the protocol to register it as a completely different block (almost certainly with an invalid proof of work) (Lewis,2015).

The block header contains the following information

- Block version number (4 bytes)
- Hash of previous block header (256 bytes)
- Hash of Merkle root (256 bytes)
- Current timestamp as seconds (4 bytes)
- Bits- storing current difficulty of network in compact format (4 bytes)
- Nonce – arbitrary number that may be used only once (4 bytes)

In blockchain network that involves mining, the POW is generally a number, called a nonce, which when combined with other data and hashed, produces a value smaller than a specified target. Computing a valid nonce takes time because there are no clues available that will lead to a sufficiently small hash, and the only approach to find one that is smaller than the target, is to compute many hashes. When a valid nonce is found, verifying it is done within a second, and then the new block propagates across the network, forming the latest consensus and blockchain. The mining process uses the hashing to make the process irreversible and faster once.

Role of Nodes in Blockchains

Any individual owning a computer can become the node of a blockchain network or can join the groups known as mining pools which forms the nodes. Moreover, the smart contract powered machines can also act as node in programmable blockchains. Simply, the node represents the entry point for individuals who wish to participate in the blockchain network. As mentioned earlier, each node in the blockchain network holds a copy of the entire public ledger similar to a local database. Every node works constantly with other nodes over a peer-to-peer network to maintain the consistency of the ledger. The transactions to be added to the chain must the entered through the nodes with the public/private key pair of the participating individuals. Generally private keys are used to sign the transactions that are addressable across the network using the corresponding public key. Use of this asymmetric key cryptography for authentication ensures integrity and non-repudiation across the blockchain network. The communications between the nodes are governed by the network protocol. Idle nodes have to burn out enough computational power to catch up with the live network and to become the part of mining process. The public ledger ensures fault tolerance as even if one node goes down or disappears, the data is never lost. The nodes thus play a vital role in making the blockchain live throughout its entire lifetime with constant interactions and computations in accordance with the prescribed consensus.

RELEVANCE OF CRYPTOGRAPHIC HASHING IN BLOCKCHAINS

In the previous section, where we discussed about the most prominent feature of blockchain – Immutability, this cannot exist as such without the support of a crisp mathematical base. Surviving the attacks and hackers in a decentralized environment will be a herculean task in any open system.

As anyone can access the blockchain network from anywhere in the world, the underlying foundation have to well-built from the grass-root level. There lies the importance of cryptographic hashing to keep each and every block tied strongly to the chain. Hashing is one of the prominent technologies in making the chain of the network and is found throughout every process in the chain. The blocks and transactions in a blockchain network are identified with the help of hashing.

Cryptographic hash functions are simple mathematical algorithms which take the input of variable size and process it into an output of fixed size, known as hash which is entirely different from the input. The most important feature of cryptographic hashing technique is that these functions can compute the output very quickly from the input provided; however no computational process should ever find the value of input from the hashed output value even if the underlying mathematical algorithm is known. Also every output value generated for a particular input value should be unique to avoid collision. Thus, even the minute changes in input values will generate an entirely different output value. Hashing algorithms thus ensure that all blocks are well formed and tamper-free, and thus the blockchain will remain secure and virtually un-breakable. Taking advantage of such characteristics, hashing can easily detect any falsification of data, and thus helps the blockchains in auditing and ensuring of the continuity of chain data and the creation of blockchains through Proof of Work utilizing the calculation of hash values. The following properties of cryptographic hashing makes the blockchain data structure functionally powerful:

1. **Easy to Generate:** It is easy to generate a hash value for a particular input using hash function.
2. **Irreversible:** It is impossible to generate original text from the hash value.
3. **Commitment:** It is not feasible to modify the original text without resulting a change in hash value thus enabling data integrity.
4. **Collision Free:** It is impossible to find two input texts that produces the same hash value

A hash function is a function that takes one piece of information of any size and maps it to another piece of data of a fixed size i.e. a 1MB file or a 500KB file when run through a hash function would produce two separate 'hashes' 128 bits in length. A Cryptographic Hash Function is one that performs this function but also fulfils three important requirements: it does so

Figure 3. Hashing process

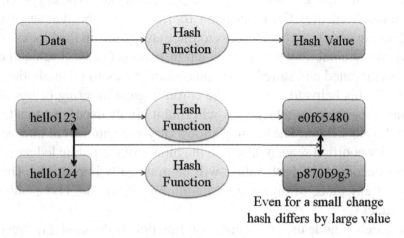

Even for a small change
hash differs by large value

in a way that no information is given on what input data produced the hash (non reversible), it does so in a way that a minor change in the input change gives a very different output hash, that the hash cannot be calculated except using the hash function (no shortcuts), that there is an extremely low probability that two different inputs will produce the same hash.

Blockchains uses the hashing technology extensively as identifiers for addresses, blocks and transactions. The blockchain addresses are generated by public key hashing as the hashing approach is collision resistant thus preventing duplicate addresses. Public-key cryptography uses different keys for encryption and decryption. The problem of handing over keys was solved by dividing the key into one for private use (private key) and one available for anyone (public key). Public-key cryptography enables safe delivery and receipt of files only if a receiver prepares a pair of a private key and a public key and delivers the public key to the sender in advance. Security of keys can be maintained even though other persons use the public key as long as the receiver properly manages his/her private key (Lewis, 2015).

Nakamoto's Bitcoin uses SHA2-256 hashing and Ethereum blockchain uses Keccak-256 hashing for signing the address of the participating nodes (Nakamoto, 2008). Every block in a blockchain are identified by its hash value which serves the purpose of identification and maintaining the integrity of the chain. Designing a secure cryptographic hashing requires good mathematical foundation and knowledge about the computational power of the computers.

In Blockchains, every node will sign each transaction with a private key before entering it into the blocks. All the participating nodes can view the contents of the transactions with the help of public key. The cryptographic key approach ensures the blockchain transactions to be tamper-proof as only genuine nodes can have access to the transactions in the blocks. These transactions are publicly verifiable and transparent. The hash value of every block is computed and stored in the succeeding block to maintain the chain sequence. This helps to maintain the chronological ordering of the blocks and ensures security as attackers would find it highly expensive to alter any data in the blockchain. The hashing allows very large number of transactions to be easily codified sequentially into the blocks of the public ledger system whereas decoding the hash values will be practically impossible. This lets us protect any piece of digital information online without bothering about future attacks.

The receiver node uses the same hash function as the sender to create the hash value of the file and compares the created hash value with the hash value obtained through decrypting the sender's digital signature with the sender's public key, thereby confirming that the sender's digital signature is authentic. This makes the system completely fool-proof and secure for any kind of transaction happening over the blockchains. Rather, the cryptographic hashing provides the much needed thrust for the security aspect of blockchains. Designing and implementing cryptographic hashing is like an art, while blockchains provides the best canvas to portray the complete potential of this masterpiece.

Figure 4. Mechanism of public-key cryptography

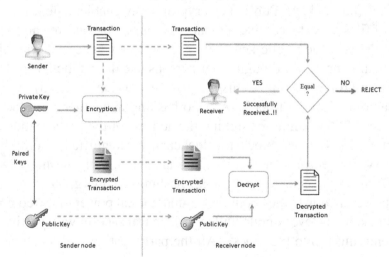

REFERENCES

Back, A. (2002). *Hashcash-a denial of service counter-measure*. Academic Press.

Biella, M. (2016). *Blockchain Technology and Applications from a Financial Perspective: Technical Report, Data & Analytics*. Coindesk.

Bitcoin Foundation Wiki. (2016). *Blockchain*. Retrieved from https://en.bitcoin.it/wiki/Block_chain

Chaum, D. (1984). Blind signature system. In Advances in cryptology (pp. 153-153). Springer US. doi:10.1007/978-1-4684-4730-9_14

Crosby, M., Pattanayak, P., Verma, S., & Kalyanaraman, V. (2016). Blockchain technology: Beyond bitcoin. *Applied Innovation*, (2), 6-10.

Jakobsson, M., & Juels, A. (1999). Proofs of work and bread pudding protocols. In Secure Information Networks (pp. 258-272). Springer US.

Lewis, A. (2015). A gentle introduction to blockchain technology. *Bits on Blocks*. Retrieved from https://bitsonblocks.net/2015/09/09/a-gentle-introduction-to-blockchain-technology/

LTP. (2016). *Know more about blockchain: Overview, technology, application areas and use cases*. Retrieved from https://letstalkpayments.com/an-overview-of-blockchain-technology/

Nakamoto, S. (2008). *Bitcoin: A peer-to-peer electronic cash system*. Academic Press.

Price, R. (2016). *Bitcoin Mining*. Retrieved from https://www.doc.ic.ac.uk/project/2015/163/g1516329/website/Proof-of-Work/proof_of_work.html

Swan, M. (2015). *Blockchain: Blueprint for a new economy*. O'Reilly Media, Inc.

Chapter 3
Advanced Topics
in Blockchains

INTRODUCTION

Even though the blockchain technology was initially proposed for the crypto-currencies, technocrats are now exploring novel areas in which the blockchain technology could do wonders. Our focus in this chapter will be to explore more into the advanced topics in the blockchain technology which will revolutionize the potential application areas in various business domains.

DISTRIBUTED PUBLIC LEDGER
SYSTEM: THE BACKBONE

Many studies forecast blockchain as a disruptive force which can replace the legacy infrastructures for storage. Vital discussions are going on around the world regarding the potential of public ledger systems as a permanent solution for record keeping. The most striking feature of blockchain that fuels discussions across enthusiasts and technocrats is the "Built-in Asset" potential of the distributed ledger. Here, every pinch of data, right from the beginning (genesis block) is wrapped up securely and sequentially into the

DOI: 10.4018/978-1-5225-2193-8.ch003

blockchain. Adding on to the authenticity, the recorded history in blockchain is mathematically verifiable at any instance of time. This leverages the immense scope of public ledgers as a safe and stable replacement for conventional storage mechanisms.

Traditional Ledger vs. Distributed Ledgers

Ledgers are the basic system of storing transaction details and record keeping from the ancient times itself. When multiple parties interact and need to keep track of complex sets of transactions people traditionally used centralized ledger. A centralized transaction ledger needs a trusted third party who makes the entries (validates), prevents double counting or double spending (safeguards), and holds the transaction histories (preserves). Public ledgers provide an open book-keeping system in which every stakeholder can update and view transactions written in the ledger. Blockchains can be viewed as a data structure that can create and share a digital ledger of transactions which is public and distributed across the entire network. In other words, the distributed public ledger system maintains the book-keeping mechanism of blockchain technology by storing every transaction written into the block and in turn storing every block forming the chain. Distributed public ledger has a considerable advantage over the conventional transaction ledgers. It is generally a tamper-proof transaction database which can be shared geographically across a large network of organizations and institutions.

Conventional ledgers mainly suffer from the problem of transaction linkage and protocol enforcement. It is generally difficult and expensive to maintain all the protocols for every entry into the ledger and also to establish connection between different transactions. Even an error in single transaction can spoil the entire balance sheets. Reconciliation and settlements make the ledgers more tedious to work on and consumes man hour. Distributed public ledger solves this problem with the blockchain network, where the chain automatically creates the link between the transactions in the chronological order. In addition, smart contracts can enforce the legal constraints as well as organizational protocol for connecting transactions and to control the limits of transaction. The nodes can follow a common protocol across the chain and the protocol will be distributed across the peer-to-peer network of blockchain. The ground breaking technology of concurrently validating transactions without any central authority, called mining, make it simpler and efficient to have any number of transactions over the decentralized platform (Kakavand

& Kost De Sevres, 2016). By potentially providing faster settlements with less error and zero reconciliation improve the business with better profit. With this public, ubiquitous ledger technology, blockchain could reduce the friction created over financial networks when different intermediaries use different technology infrastructures.

In a generic terminology, distributed public ledgers are simply a huge spreadsheet that runs on thousands of computers across the world which allows anonymous people to share data safely without bothering about trust. Every participant in the network will hold the identical copy of the ledger, with every modification in the ledger reflecting to all the copies within the least time. Even though the distributed ledgers are open and public, it is practically impossible to modify a transaction stored in the blockchain (Wall Street Journal, 2014).

The cryptographic approaches used in blockchains provide private-public key pairs to provide identity abstraction across the public ledgers. Accordingly, the identities of the individuals participating as nodes are never revealed and only the security keys (Private-public keys) are used for transactions. Only the nodes with valid private key can initiate a transaction and the participating nodes with corresponding public keys can gain output. The identity abstraction feature provides authorization as well as authentication to nodes of the network.

Figure 1. Elements of distributed public ledger

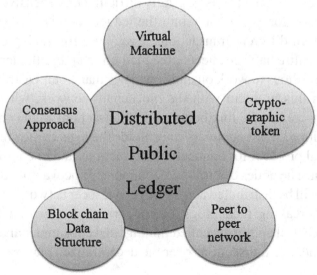

Tamper-Proof Ledgers

The Blockchain technology can have a disruptive revolution in distributed ledger technology which is still in infancy. The Blockchain technology which creates and adds blocks to the existing chain allows any node in the network to add transactions into the public ledger, provided they can solve the computational puzzle for the same. This chain of blocks containing the successful transactions will create a distributed public ledger which works in a trust-free manner over the network. In future, public blockchains can create smart contract based permission-less ledgers in which anyone can add transactions that solves the POW on the network. Smart contracts can easily control the ledger entries and assign the rules for transactions. The distributed public ledgers are now preferred over centralized databases as they are inherently harder to attack as the attacker needs to modify all the multiple copies of blockchain located at multiple locations over the network at the same time, which is practically impossible (DTCC, 2016). Blockchain technology also makes the public ledger tamper-proof as the modification in the ledger requires very high computational cost to redo the consensus protocol and achieve the successful proof-of-work.

Figure 2. How public ledgers are made tamper-proof

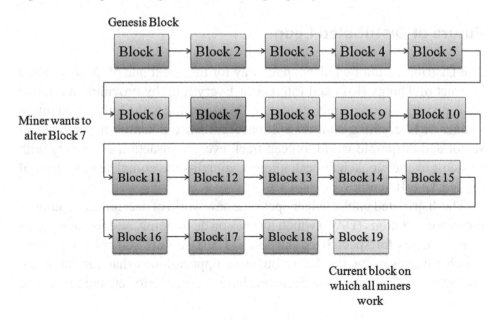

31

In the above figure, a blockchain is illustrated with every miner working on building the block number 19. If a miner wants to modify an intermediate block, say Block 7, the miner have to make the modification in transaction data of Block 7 and recreate the chain from Block 7 – 18. All these have to happen within a limited time in which the Block 19 is being mined by other miners. This makes it practically impossible to tamper the data in public ledgers stored over blockchain

The Public ledger technology also improves the potential of distributed work environment and in future it can disrupt the need for corporate offices and work-spaces as anyone can perform transactions from anywhere in the world. This can also avoid much of the paper-work and hefty record keeping process. In future, even the data warehouses will be converted to blockchain based distributed ledgers. Eventually, it will also provide new disruptions in data pooling and file duplication and avoids unnecessary redundancies in the prevailing systems. Only one copy of one file is required for the entire public ledger. As record keeping makes an unavoidable part of any business, the distributed public ledger has huge potential for disruption in almost every industry in the world. Distributed ledgers promote trading of anything value-based over the network by providing a permanent and secure tool which does not requires a centralized control. This makes the trading cheaper and faster through the secure public ledgers. Blockchain enthusiasts even predict the possibility of a single global distributed ledger in the coming future which covers up all the transactions happening across the world.

Future of Distributed Ledgers

The Distributed public ledgers pave way for the backbone of Decentralized Internet of Things (IoT) and Internet of Everything by providing a reliable backend which can securely store everything coming to the Internet. In future Ledger of Everything concept will have immense potential in government sector and corporate world to keep track every transaction efficiently with less cost as the blockchain technology maintains the complete audit trail of the blocks efficiently.

The distributed public ledger opens the new world of decentralized autonomous organizations (DAO) which focuses on developing autonomous agents and processes for specialized purposes. The DAO are self-reliant systems which paves way for the future business opportunities that can automate every process and take wise decisions based on scenarios encountered. The transparency needed for DAO transactions are incorporated by the public ledgers with better integrity among the participating nodes. This also reduces the overhead of audit and chances of disputes over transactions.

Distributed ledgers will revolutionize the governmental tasks like issuing passports, collecting taxes, voting system, public distribution systems (PDS), delivering grants and other benefits, record land registries etc. This provides better monitoring and controlling and ensures integrity among the various governmental services. Distributed ledgers help the government to ensure personal attention for every citizen of the nation in an organized and efficient manner and to resolve the public grievances through the consensus approach. The citizens will have the advantage of getting individual preferences and needs with the embedded smart contracts. The Smart contracts will power the distributed ledgers to reduce the complexity and improves the efficiency of delivering services.

EXPLORING THE BLOCKCHAIN CONSENSUS STRATEGY

Consensus is an ancient strategy adopted by mankind for taking collective decisions over a problem. The key focus was on 'consent' made by every person to follow a procedure. Before the rise of dictatorship and governments, ancient tribes followed the consensus approach in which the decision approved by the majority have to be accepted by all the group members. This was considered as an efficient approach to solve disputes and to generate wise decisions. Consensus refers to a collective task where every participating individual expresses their view regarding a scenario. Eventually, these views will be synthesized to generate the best possible strategy for the scenario at the given instant. Generally, the individuals can agree or disagree over a scenario but the outcome generated based on the best need of the group at that instant. Voting is one the common and most popular approach to achieve consensus.

Consensus Strategy is used in blockchain technology to securely maintain the immutable history of transactions without the help of a trusted third party. An important function of consensus is to protect against attacks on the blockchain and to reach consensus in case multiple instances of the blockchain appear. This makes the distributed public ledger tamper-proof as well as transparent. According to 'The Economist', the intermediary banks across the world charged an estimated 1.7 trillion US dollars as fee for processing payments in 2014 which accounts to about 2% of entire world economy.

With blockchain, lot of this money can be saved as it eliminates the need of intermediaries.

Consensus plays a major role in financial services, where trades and transactions are often verified by a central clearinghouse that maintains its own central ledger. Usually this process take days to settle a transaction, and the clearinghouse typically collects some kind of fee. Blockchain technology could eliminate that clearinghouse by giving each bank in the network its own copy of the ledger. A common network protocol and consensus mechanism would allow the participants to communicate with one another. Using this method, transactions could be approved automatically in seconds or minutes, significantly cutting costs and boosting efficiency (Bitcoin.org, 2009).

Vitalik Buterin, (Founder of Ethereum) describes that the purpose of a consensus algorithm is to allow for the secure updating of a state according to some specific state transition rules, where the right to perform the state transitions is distributed among the economic set. The economic set can be users which are given the right to collectively perform transitions through an algorithm. According to him, the mechanism behind proof of work was a breakthrough because it simultaneously solved two problems. First, it provided a simple and moderately effective consensus algorithm, allowing nodes in the network to collectively agree on a set of updates to the state of the Bitcoin ledger. Second, it provided a mechanism for allowing free entry into the consensus process, solving the political problem of deciding who gets to influence the consensus, while simultaneously preventing sybil attacks. It does this by substituting a formal barrier to participation, such as the requirement to be registered as a unique entity on a particular list, with an economic barrier - the weight of a single node in the consensus voting process is directly proportional to the computing power that the node brings (Buterin, 2013a).

With the consensus strategy, the Blockchain technology can effectively solve the concurrency problem in a completely distributed manner. Instead of having a central authority that maintains a database and guards its authenticity, a copy of the entire database is distributed to every node in the network. These nodes follow the consensus protocol and compare their versions together through a continuous process of "voting". The version that gets the most votes from the network is accepted as authentic, and the process repeats indefinitely.

As seen in the Bitcoin mechanism, to get active participation of the nodes of the blockchain, an incentive mechanism is included in the consensus: Voting with the majority, which is being accepted by all the nodes across the network as authentic will be rewarded as incentives, while voting against the majority rule will be penalized. This creates a healthy gaming scenario where all the participants play fair to anticipate each other's choices and try to upvote for the version that will eventually be accepted through the consensus.

This incentive-based consensus scenario will eliminate the need for a central authority to maintain every transaction in proper order and to enforce rules of the network. In blockchain network, every node tends to maintain the history of transactions for the validation process and works on a peer-to-peer server-less platform to achieve the consensus strategy. This creates a new way of managing data over trust-free incentivized work platform over the distributed public ledger.

Working of Proof of Work

As discussed earlier, Proof of Work (POW) is a verification process that involves solving a complex set of algorithms requiring a significant amount of computational power. Proof-of-Work is one of the most commonly used consensus approach for blockchains. The miner starts to build a candidate block filled with all the raw transactions competing to be added to the block-chain. The miner then computes the hash value of his block header and checks whether it matches the current target value. If the hash value does not match, it will modify the nonce, usually through adding one to it, and then repeat the process. It is virtually impossible to fetch two different inputs having the same result after cryptographic hashing as the output of the cryptographic hash function changes drastically when there is a minor change to the input. Blockchains generally uses one-way Elliptic Curve Cryptography for ensuring the credibility. A nonce is an arbitrary number that may only be used once. Blockchain uses a nonce to tune the difficulty of solving the hashing function.

The blockchain network is collaboratively maintained by anonymous peers on the network, such that each block have to invest a significant amount of work in its creation to ensure that untrustworthy peers who want to modify past blocks have to work harder than honest peers who only want to add new blocks to the blockchain.

The process of creating the chain of blocks in the chronological order makes it impossible to modify transactions included in any block without modifying all the succeeding blocks. As a result, the cost to modify a particular block increases with every new block added to the blockchain, magnifying the effect of the proof of work.

Figure 3. Flow diagram of proof of work mechanism

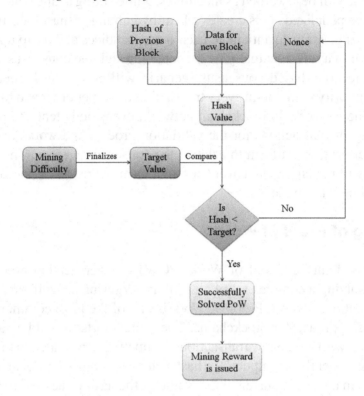

According to the Developer Guide issued by Bitcoin.org, in the blockchain network every node have to prove that it performed a specific amount of work to create a block and have to create a hash of the block header which should be within the specific limits (Bitcoin.org, 2009). For example, if the maximum possible hash value is $2^{256} - 1$, you can prove that you tried up to two combinations by producing a hash value less than 2^{255}.

The new blocks will only be added to the block chain if their hash is at least as challenging as a difficulty value expected by the consensus protocol. According to the developers theory, for every 2016 blocks, the blockchain network uses timestamps stored in each block header to calculate the number of seconds elapsed between generation of the first and last of those last 2016 blocks. The ideal value is 1,209,600 seconds (two weeks). Generally, if the time taken to generate 2,016 blocks is less than two weeks, the expected difficulty value is increased proportionally (by as much as 300%) so that the next 2,016 blocks should take exactly two weeks to generate if hashes are checked at the same rate. If it took more than two weeks to generate the blocks, the expected difficulty value is decreased proportionally (by as much as 75%) for the same reason (Bitcoin.org, 2009).

As mentioned in previous chapter, in the Bitcoin blockchain, the proof of work is generally termed as mining. The nodes of bitcoin network calculate a hash value by adding a nonce (any given value) to the collection of transaction data delivered to them. After computation, the nodes should obtain a value smaller than a certain value, and the nodes have to continue calculations by using different nonces until they obtain the required value. The condition is that the double-SHA256 hash of every block, treated as a 256-bit number, must be less than a dynamically adjusted target. The purpose of this is to make block creation computationally "hard", thereby preventing sybil attackers from remaking the entire blockchain in their favor. As the SHA256 algorithm will provide a completely unpredictable pseudorandom function, the only method to create a valid block is "trial and error method", repeatedly by incrementing the nonce and comparing whether the new hash matches the older one. Whenever any node gets the desired value, all the participating nodes agrees upon the correctness of the value and the collection of transaction data used for the calculations is approved to be official transaction results as a new block.

Finally, bitcoins are granted as a reward to the person who succeeded in obtaining the correct value through the calculations. After that, all participants go on to the next mining using transaction data that were not included in said block and the newly created transaction data. Satoshi proposed the One CPU/ One Vote concept for the POW of Bitcoin Blockchain to make it a fair play for all the participating nodes.

The proof of work used in Bitcoin blockchain takes advantage of the apparently random nature of cryptographic hashes. As we had seen earlier, a good cryptographic hash algorithm converts the input data into some random combination of alphanumerical. Whenever the data gets modified through any operation, a new combination is generated by the hash function, which makes it practically impossible to modify the data to make the hash number predictable. But the transactions on the Bitcoin blockchain often take a hour or more to get completed and require large amounts of electricity via miners who verify transactions. In future, this enormous power consumption and time delay will be major hindrance form using the proof of work for financial and non financial applications. So, people started thinking about faster and efficient methods like Proof of stake and Proof of existence which could save money and time.

Proof of Stake (POS)

According to Bitcoin magazine, the number of computations happening in Bitcoin network per second is six hundred trillion SHA256 computations and basically these computations have no practical or scientific value; their only purpose is to solve proof of work problems that are deliberately made to be hard so that malicious attackers cannot easily pretend to be millions of nodes and overpower the network. Even though it is wastage of precious time and computational power the users are left with no other options in initial period to transfer digital currency across the world without any intermediaries. Later, several other consensus strategies were developed and Proof of Stake (POS) was one of them. Proof of Stake was developed as an alternative for Proof of Work with reduced computations and less constraints for generation of blocks. Since POW required huge computational power, nodes with high-end GPU miners had an advantage of mining blocks over the regular nodes. Even though it would be costlier effort, this created a possibility for hacker groups for winning the consensus if they can deploy large number of enormous GPUs to gain control over the blockchain network from the valid miners (Buterin, 2013b).

In POS, instead of mining power, the probability to create a block and receive the associated reward is proportional to a user's ownership stake in the system. Any individual who have 'n' percentage of total stake creates a new block with probability 'n'. In other words, the owners of major shares have an advantage over the others in creating the new block. The crux of proof of stake that the individuals with the highest stakes in the system have the most interest to maintain a secure network, as they will suffer the most if the reputation and price of the system would diminish because of the attacks. Gaining the stake to obtain authority will be an expensive affair for the attacker and the chances obtaining stake from legitimate owners/individuals are very low.

SCOPE OF TRUST-FREE ENVIRONMENT

Transparency and security combine to form a major disruption that makes blockchain a completely trust-free technology. Blockchains redefines how trust is perceived in a digital environment. The reason why blockchain technology is considered so disruptive is that it has the ability to solve this problem of authenticity without the inclusion of any trusted intermediaries. Blockchain is secure through the immutability it gains from the hashing algorithms, when applied on the decentralized network, and transparent because anyone can look through all blocks. In essence, blockchains have introduced a completely new type of digital trust which manifests itself in a fully distributed way without anyone having to trust any single member of the network (Mougayar, 2015). The only trust required is in that, on average, the participants of the network are behaving honestly — or more to the point, that the majority of the entire network is not colluding against the others in a coordinated manner.

From the time of inception, the computer networks are always in constant fear of attacks and intruders. Trust among the nodes of the network plays a crucial role when the network deals with anonymous entities. Whooping amount of money are spent on security systems and trusted third-parties to ensure security to the network as more and more security threats are emerging day by day. The trust in computing is becoming serious issue in most of the critical areas which hindrances many business capabilities.

The blockchain technology makes a disruption in the trusted computing by providing a trustless/ trust-free computing paradigm which eliminates the need for a trusted-third party. Rather than increasing the security measures and innovating on trusted platforms, blockchain simply eliminates the need for a trusted platform. Blockchain makes it possible for users to interact with any anonymous entity in the network without any concern over the identity of the participating node. It allows anyone to verify the authenticity of transaction and data independently, without considering some others opinion, irrespective of whom or where that data came from in the network. It provides security and privacy to both the users and data being handled over blockchain. The blockchain uses the cryptographic hash address for every user and does not reveal the actual identity of anyone across the chain which makes the personal information secure and hidden. With this, we do not need to trust anyone on the chain as trust is incorporated by the chain in its implementation itself. The data once stored in blocks through consensus approach becomes immutable and the owner of data can assure that the data remains tamper-proof.

FREEDOM OF DECENTRALIZED ENVIRONMENT

We have also discussed the potential of decentralized platforms over centralized ones on the first chapter. Blockchain technology can be viewed as "The Best"

Decentralization Approach currently available in the world. Decentralization process allows the computing to enjoy the freedom of autonomous components delivering preferred services by its own. The autonomous components can enhance the reach of computational power beyond a centralized server and provides exponential growth for the concerned businesses. The dictatorship of master servers in centralized computing made hindrances for localized computing and expansion of networks to adapt new business scenarios. Decentralized computing provides better adaptability to the ground reality with faster expansion or contraction of components to cope up with the needs of the economy. This improves the availability of resources over a wide network with better reliability and less down-time. Specialized computations can also be incorporated with local autonomy for handling unique use cases. Concurrent resource utilization and parallel processing capabilities of decentralized platforms helps to ease the computational process and reduce the overburden on resources. Autonomous components help in quicker migration and restructuring in case of emergencies and can perform efficiently by integrating with available connection points. This can ensure better performance and reduces the cost of computing.

VARIANTS OF BLOCKCHAINS

Different variants of blockchain with different consensus approaches and different public ledger structures are used, depending on the type and size of the network and the use case of a particular company. The initial bitcoin blockchain is public and permission-less, which means anyone can participate in the network and contribute to the ledger. Most of the crypto-currency blockchains require public blockchains for adding and removing nodes from time to time. For a closed scenario, most of the firms are also exploring the potential of private or permissioned blockchains. Here the network will be made up of known nodes with restriction and rules on adding new nodes (Lewis, 2015). Different implementations of blockchains behave in different manner based on the underlying smart contract.

Public Blockchains

Nakamoto's paper on Bitcoin refers to the creation to the creation of a public blockchain where anyone on the platform can become a blockchain node would be able to read or write to the platform, provided they work on the consensus strategy for the same. Most of the blockchain application uses the public blockchain as large number of users can participate in the network easily. Also, a public blockchain is considered to be a fully decentralized blockchain. Few public blockchain platforms are:

- **Ethereum:** A provider of a decentralized platform and programming language that helps running smart contracts and allows developers to publish distributed applications.
- **Factom:** A provider of records management, records business processes for business and governments.
- **Blockstream:** A provider of sidechain technology, focused on extending capabilities of bitcoin. The company has started experimenting on providing accounting (considered a function to be done on private blockchain) with the use of public blockchain technology.

Private Blockchains

A private blockchain, on the other hand, allows only the owner to have the rights on any changes that have to be done. This could be seen as a similar version to the existing infrastructure wherein the owner (a centralized authority) would have the power to change the rules, revert transactions, etc. based on the need. It could find use cases to build proprietary systems and reduce the costs while at the same time; increase their efficiency (Lewis, 2015). Private blockchains helps to maintain the organizational hierarchy and can instill protocols of the Some of the examples could be:

- **Eris Industries:** A provider of shared software database using blockchain technology.
- **Blockstack:** A provider of financial institutions back office operations, including clearing & settlement on a private blockchain.
- **Multichain:** Provides an open source distributed database for financial transactions.
- **Chain Inc.:** A provider of blockchain APIs. Chain partnered with Nasdaq OMX Group Inc., to provide a platform that enables trading private company shares with the blockchain.

Hybrid/Consortium Blockchains

The concept of Hybrid blockchain arises from the use-cases having combination of private and public blockchain. These blockchains will provide write access to limited number of nodes like the private blockchain and these can be shared across different domains within the organization or outside to form a public blockchain. Here the consensus is maintained among a predefined group of nodes and the read privilege will be same as that of a public blockchain. Hybrid blockchains explore the potential of data sharing among a large community with proper restrictions and regulations as of a private blockchain (Lewis,2015).

BLOCKCHAIN USE-CASES

From the time of inception, majority of use-cases in blockchain were in payments and financial settlements. Blockchain has made waves by showing a valuable contribution to the financial services industry as it provides the evidence of the activity, trades and transfers on the network. Later on, non-financial use-cases started flourishing by the era of Blockchain 2.0. The current non-financial uses cases mainly focus on digital asset handling, decentralized internet of things, identity management, smart contract development and documentary trade. It will be quite fascinating to see how these use cases are being adopted by governments and the public sector alike to streamline processes, thereby improving the life of the masses. Some of the key area where Blockchain plays disruption includes Contract and document management and digitalization, Supply chain monitoring, Prediction markets, Electronic voting systems, Counterfeit prevention for digital assets and proof of ownership, Governance, Escrow service, Ride sharing, Decentralized cloud storage, App Development etc. (LTP, 2016). Blockchain offers limitless opportunities to develop solutions for every possible business need. In the chapters 6 and 7, we will be discussing the above mentioned use cases and the upcoming trends in leveraging blockchain technology in various business domains.

REFERENCES

Bitcoin.org. (2009). *Bitcoin Developer Guide*. Retrieved from https://bitcoin. org/en/developer-guide

Buterin, V. (2013a). *Ethereum white paper*. Ethereum.

Buterin, V. (2013b). *What Proof of Stake is and Why it Matters*. bitcoin-magazine.com.

DTCC. (2016). *Embracing Disruption: Tapping The Potential Of Distributed Ledgers To Improve The Post-Trade Landscape*. Retrieved from https://www. finextra.com/finextra-downloads/newsdocs/embracing%20disruption%20 white%20paper_final_jan-16.pdf

Kakavand, H., & Kost De Sevres, N. (2016). *The Blockchain Revolution: An Analysis of Regulation and Technology Related to Distributed Ledger Technologies*. Academic Press.

Lewis, A. (2015). A gentle introduction to blockchain technology. *Bits on Blocks*. Retrieved from https://bitsonblocks.net/2015/09/09/a-gentle-intro-duction-to-blockchain-technology/

LTP. (2016). *Know more about blockchain: Overview, technology, applica-tion areas and use cases*. Retrieved from https://letstalkpayments.com/an-overview-of-blockchain-technology/

Mougayar, W. (2015). *Understanding the blockchain*. Retrieved from https:// www.oreilly.com/ideas/understanding-the-blockchain

Swan, M. (2015). *Blockchain: Blueprint for a new economy*. O'Reilly Media, Inc.

Wall Street Journal. (2014). *The Imminent Decentralized Computing Revolu-tion*. Retrieved from http://blogs.wsj.com/accelerators/2014/10/10/weekend-read-the-imminent-decentralized-computing-revolution/

Chapter 4
Smart Contracts and Smart Properties Over Blockchains

INTRODUCTION TO SMART CONTRACTS

In everyday life of humans, contracts are valuable mechanisms to uphold the promises between known or unknown individuals in a fair manner. By definition, a contract is a voluntary agreement between two or more parties creating certain obligations enforceable by law. Contracts are generally enforced to ensure smooth interaction with all the stake holders over the participating scenario without any problems and minimal need of trust. The beauty of a contract is that you have a remedy when people break their promises. By incorporating the power of physical contracts into the computing world, we could create wonders in the way we do businesses with clearly outlined contractual terms and solve disputes, if any, amicably. With all the noteworthy properties of blockchain network, it turns out that blockchain seems to be the perfect platform for deploying the digital contracts to run digital businesses than making physical contracts to run digital businesses. This thought gave rise to the invention of smart contracts, the programmable digital contracts

DOI: 10.4018/978-1-5225-2193-8.ch004

written and deployed using any turing complete language over the blockchain network (Buterin, 2014).

Smart Contracts are self-executing programs which run on the blockchain and are capable of enforcing rules, consequences and computation over every transaction happening in the blockchain. The concept of smart contracts was first formally coined by Nick Szabo in 1994. Smart contracts can take any form of data as input; perform computations over the input based on the protocols specified in the smart contract and can enforce decisions based on the prevailing conditions for producing the output (Szabo, 1997). This revolutionary concept automates the enforcement of contractual promises without any intermediaries or trusted-third parties and improves transparency as every individual node in the blockchain abides the protocols specified in the smart contract. All the contract transactions are stored in blockchain in a chronological order for future access along with the complete audit trail of events. Also the participating nodes cannot tamper or change the contract agreements stored in the blockchain thus removing the chances of attack. Smart contracts make the entire network behave like a large central computer, but avoid the risk of failures, cost and trust of a centralized computing mechanism.

Like any regular legal contract or agreement, smart contract can incorporate every possible consequence of transaction behavior and can issue the actions to be taken for each scenario. Smart contracts makes it possible to deal with all the valid and invalid transactions that can happen over a blockchain and even trace out abnormal actions from participating nodes. The smart contracts does not store any data, instead they provide a guideline on how the data are stored in blockchain. Rather, they have the potential to reduce and even eliminate the chances of fraud and overhead costs of many commercial transactions.

Consider a simple example of supply chain which is currently controlled by the intermediaries mostly through a centralized platform. We have chosen this sample scenario since the supply chain is a major business scenario where middlemen play a major role in controlling the activities right from the production to distribution. Many unlawful activities like hoarding, black marketing etc. happens in the supply chains to multiply the profits of middleman and the producers and customers suffer a lot. Before unveiling the blockchain platform, it was practically impossible to administer and govern the individual activities over the Internet without the help of a centralized governing organization which ensures that the data is not getting tampered or fudged by any attacker. Due to lack of a stable decentralized platform the independent individuals could not confirm that a transaction had successfully being performed without relying on a trusted central body to verify that this particular transaction was genuine.

The middleman, who plays an economic role intermediate in the society in controlling the business between producers and consumers for decades, will get eliminated by the potential of smart contract powered blockchains. Moreover, it provides liberty for people to perform transactions of digital assets or data across the blockchain network, in a secure, trust-free, and immutable way. It could do wonders in the supply chain by enabling a legal set of protocols for every transactions happening in the supply chain. Moreover, the public ledger system may enhance visibility and thus fair distribution and pricing to products with lesser wastages.

Need for Smart Contracts

The evolution of autonomous scripts for handling any kind of business or process based upon the digital assets stored in the blockchain which can self-execute, self-verify, self-enforce and self-constrain the agreement between two parties give rise to the thought of smart contracts. The role of the blockchain network is to eliminate the need of a trusted third party for resolving any kind legal disputes that may arise between the participants of the contract. The modular and repeatable smart contracts enable the building of applications for specific use-cases and are encoded into the blockchain at specific address known as contract address, which is determined at the time

Figure 1. How smart contracts eliminate middleman in supply chain

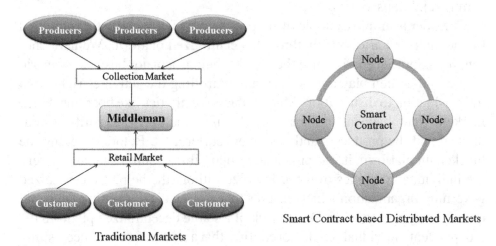

of deployment. Whenever the nodes initiate an activity being controlled by the smart contract, a transaction is sent to the contract address and the virtual machine executes the contract code using the data input from the transaction. In other words, smart contracts are self-executing applications that run exactly as programmed with zero downtime, censorship, fudging or third party interference (Buterin, 2014).

Smart contracts avoid the delays and expenses incurred by physical contracts. They can execute independently without the influence of any external entities and have the potential to take necessary actions during the events of violation of contract. Generally, the promises are hardwired into the code to create an "unbreakable" contract. Such contracts will have zero flexibility and will stick on its motto. New programming language like Solidity, Serpent etc. are designed for writing smart contracts which can precisely specify the outcomes with zero ambiguity in contract interpretations and can refrain any sort of violation. By agreeing to use a smart contract, the participating individuals effectively cede control over an aspect of the performance of a contractual obligation to a digitized process which cannot be reasoned with or influenced.

Implementation of Smart Contracts

For obtaining the desired functionalities, smart contracts needs to be implemented by clearly specifying every aspect of the system. Technically, a smart contract is a program code written using any Ethereum compatible language, that the Ethereum Virtual Machine (EVM) (will be explained in the coming chapter) is able to execute over the blockchain. Once the program code has been added to the blockchain as bytecode, the smart contract itself cannot be modified or decoded back to readable format. After this, the nodes can only perform storage and retrieval operation on the immutable contract code (Luu et al., 2016). The smart contracts deployed over the Ethereum blockchain network will have a unique contract address and is available globally to any node over the network. A Smart contract can simply invoke other smart contracts using message call statements. According of Vitalik Buterin (Founder of Ethereum), the total computational power available on the blockchain network is more or less similar to that of a smartphone of late 90's. But still, the smart contracts are highly powerful in building the decentralized platforms for trust-free networks across the world. Smart contracts are realized by the turing complete programming languages that can convert the contract into bytecode and finally execute them using EVM. Currently available programming languages that supports Ethereum platform are Solidity (Java like), Serpent (Python like), Mutan (C like), and LLL (Lisp like). Even though each smart contract has a contract address to uniquely identify the contract globally, it differs from the bitcoin wallet in the fact that it can execute the contract code based on the data received through transactions. For resisting different forms of attacks like DDoS, malicious codes, infinite loop problems, every step involved in creation and execution of smart contract involves spending of certain amount of virtual currency, simply termed as gas or ether (hence known as Ethereum). The total number of computations and data storage entries of the contract byte code generated by the EVM compiler determines the amount of gas require to run the entire smart contract.

The gas price determines the cost of every action to be performed during the execution of EVM bytecode and making transactions over the blockchain. The gas acts as fuel for running the contracts and every node should possess sufficient fuel to run the smart contract. Usually the computational complexity of statements defines the gas needed for its executions. The simple mathematical computations such as addition, subtraction, and multiplication will cost 1 gas for every instance of execution. Generally, a start price is set for every smart contract to pay reward to every miner for the computational power being spent by them. The gas prices are restricted only to transactions in the smart contracts while the messages send between different contracts does not require gas for communication. The total amount of gas being spent all the executions done of all the smart contracts initiated by any transaction should in the limits of the gas field of the corresponding transaction. Otherwise, abnormal termination of executions may arise due to exhausting of gas. Generally, a well – defined mathematical logic should be incorporated into every contract for proper estimation and utilization of gas and to deal with any critical situation such that the contract remains live globally to every participating node

Applications of Smart Contracts

1. Smart contracts facilitated rental and lease services will be creating disruption in the coming era. A simple digital key controlled by a smart contract can be used to lease vehicles, house, rooms and other services to customers without the burden of handling the service manually. IoT powered smart control is emerging which helps to lease any service

remotely without any caretaker or issuing authority. Slock.it had demonstrated a smart lock powered with IoT and blockchain technology that be used to rent house and rooms based on smart contracts. Access to rooms will be disabled automatically after the specific usage time through these smart contracts. Airbnb, a peer-to-peer online homestay reservation network is also experimenting the potential of smart contracts for leasing rooms. IBM Blockchain has demonstrated smart contract based car rental services with significant reduction in overhead costs and offers higher integrity and security.

2. Smart contracts could bring tremendous changes in the e-commerce business by enabling autonomous digital markets where any individual can buy or sell anything without the need of intermediary business portals. This can reduce the market complexities and delays and helps governments for better taxation through the public ledger support. IoT powered drones are also being tested currently for door step delivery of goods to ensure on-time and secure delivery (Sofia, 2016).

3. In the field of machine-to-machine (M2M) communication and machine learning, Smart contracts can bring out extraordinary capabilities for device interaction and automation to a level perceivable by humans. Self driving vehicles, autonomous gadgets and Self equipped devices (like ADEPT) could be realized effectively with the immense potential of smart contracts (Sofia, 2016).

4. Any case where the value needs to be released upon met conditions is an area of a smart contract application. Funding (scholarship, discount, sponsorship, donation, etc.) can be automatically released once the conditions for each case are met and verified digitally. Digitally executed due diligence for startups can automatically release the funds as a final step of an investment.

5. In future, even the betting and gambling will be powered with blockchain-enabled smart contracts to avoid frauds to make it legal. Smart contracts will be enabled to find the winners and to pay rewards based on the play statistics.

6. The property rights and transfer of assets to legal heirs can be digitalized with the smart contracts to enable much complex legal documents or escrow statements. This can also automate the asset transfer to concerned parties when the owner gets deceased.

Potential Challenges in Building Smart Contracts

One of the major challenges of smart contracts will be the acceptance of digital code in the physical world. The current physical world have to adapt to the contract code amicably with human consensus. According to Sofia, there are three possible solutions for this task: multi-signature transactions, prediction markets and oracles.

Multi-signature transactions unveil the idea of trust agent to be involved to confirm on the conditions for triggering the contract between the parties have been met and the contract can be executed.

The core idea of Prediction market is that the public can make a more accurate prediction of the events than a single expert. While building prediction on certain events, with some economic incentive, crowds can be involved in providing a genuine opinion. The economic incentive can be built in a way so that it rewards the most accurate prediction. Hence, the crowd will be incentivized to act as accurate as possible.

Augur is an example of such a project. Augur is an Ethereum-based decentralized prediction market that brings together three core elements into one beautiful solution: the wisdom of the crowds powering prediction markets that are decentralized.

Oracle is the third possible solution for triggering digital events from a physical world. Oracle services are defined as third-parties that are verifying the outcome of the events and feed the data to smart contracts data services. However, there is a problem with oracles themselves. Who can ensure the trustworthiness of an oracle? The Oracle may draw the result from an infinite network, but where is the guarantee that even if each node can be trusted, the result is correct and can be trusted as well?

Opportunities in Smart Contracts

With the advent of blockchain 2.0, the programmable smart contracts made a tremendous growth from transaction management to even the autonomous governance. From the simple value exchange protocols and DAOs, Smart contracts pave way for the development of some of the novel concepts like Distributed Autonomous Society (DAS) and Distributed Autonomous Governments which could revolutionize the existing governance and political scenario to a more democratic level giving at most consideration the needs of every individual in the society. It will help business to gain more customers and meet client needs quickly and efficiently. In short, in the coming future smart contracts with its unimaginable potential will be a disruptive factor in various domains of human life

POTENTIAL OF SMART PROPERTIES

The blockchains can handle any form of tangible and intangible assets over various business scenarios. These assets will be transferred across numerous stakeholders over different market places. The functionalities of these blockchain-based assets will be specified as smart properties which can be controlled by smart contracts. Smart properties are functionalities that have to be performed while smart contracts satisfy certain conditions. It defines the behavior of every digital asset to its stake holder minimizing the chance of conflicts over its usage and application. These smart properties might be realized by incorporating the smart contracts on the physical and digital assets controlled over blockchain network (Wagner, 2016).

Every digital asset over the blockchain can be powered with smart properties to reduce the need of trust. The cryptographic private key of the asset plays a major role in controlling ownership and access rights of digital asset over blockchains. The owner can sell the asset to another person by transferring the private key. For example, the smart property will be a car knowing its owner and enable only the legitimate owner to access the car preventing theft. The smart contract can control these smart properties to transfer the ownership of car to another person only on the basis of stipulated rules. This involves transfer of private key from previous owner to the current one through the agreement defined in smart contracts. For example, if a person took loan for purchasing a new car and fails to make monthly repayment, the smart contracts can initiate process to stop accessing the car by the owner who made default and lien the car.

The Idea of Smart Properties

The core idea of smart properties is the affirmation of ownership rights for an asset digitally through its entry into the blockchain's immutable public ledger, using the private key of the owner. The asset owner having private key can ascertain its ownership with corresponding public key to other individuals. Whenever the owner decides to sell the asset, the smart contract completes the process by handing over the owner's private key to the buyer. Some types of property like trademarks, copyrights and patents are inherently smart properties, and their management as such is natural and can be fruitful. Indeed these entitlements can be easily encoded and processed as digital documents. This is not the case with physical assets, where ownership is more exposed to frauds. In fact in order to register a chattel (e.g a car) in the blockchain, we need to attach a uniquely identifiable tag or a chip to it. If the information contained in that tag or chip could be altered, or the tag/chip could be detached, smart property would not be guaranteed.

One of the actual implementation of smart properties is colored coins. Colored coin is simply an open source protocol which helps in creating and managing digital assets on top of the Bitcoin Blockchain. This protocol extends the possibilities of bitcoin blockchain beyond currency aspect by including a class of methods that helps users to correlate the real world assets to the blockchain network. Colored coins work by attaching the metadata to the transactions of bitcoin blockchain and utilize the blockchain network for issuing and transfer of assets. In fact it is possible to store smaller pieces of metadata on the bitcoin blockchain to represent asset manipulation instructions (Wagner, 2016). One can encode in a Bitcoin transaction the information that some units of a new asset were issued and credited to a given Bitcoin address, and a real world value can correspond to those units with the issuer's promise to redeem them for some goods or services. The colored coins are applied in wide array of applications like proving ownership with digital keys (for issuing digital key to vehicles, apartments, lockers etc.), digital lockers for storage (like movies, audio, documents, certificates) or designing smart contracts for financial transaction.

TURING COMPLETE PROGRAMMING: ETHEREUM

The Ethereum project was formally announced by Vitalik Buterin in January 2014 at the The North American Bitcoin Conference in Miami, Florida, USA. Vitalik Buterin was a developer associated with Bitcoin and published a white paper about the Ethereum "A Next Generation Smart Contract & Decentralized Application Platform" in the late 2013 which describes about developing the decentralized applications (Dapps) on Ethereum platform (Buterin, 2014). Later, in the early 2014, Dr. Gavin Wood associated with Buterin and co-founded Ethereum. The Ethereum Yellow Paper was released by Gavin in April 2014. The yellow paper described in depth about the Ethereum Virtual

Machine (EVM) which could be used as the backbone of smart contracts and Dapps (Wood, 2014). Ethereum was the first turing complete platform for developing programmable blockchains that could revolutionize the development of decentralized applications. Buterin considered Ethereum as the next generation decentralized application platform which have immense potential to develop more Bitcoin-like applications in the decentralized environment. This concept is clearly specified by Buterin in the Ethereum white paper as he suggests Ethereum as an 'alternate protocol' for developing Dapps. He mainly focuses on getting faster application development time with high security and better interaction among the Dapps. The Ethereum project realizes this by building the base layer, the open blockchain platform with a built in turing-complete programming language that helps programmers to write smart contracts that are executable directly over the blockchain. Moreover, wide variety of Dapps can be directly integrated on top of the blockchain platform that is secure and powerful. The most striking feature of programmable blockchain like Ethereum project is that it can disrupt potentially every business domain with the advent of Dapps.

The token used in Ethereum blockchain is known as Ether, which is used for paying transaction fee over the Ethereum network. Ether is also considered as a crypto-currency like Bitcoin and is now traded for reasonable value over the crypto-currency exchanges. The crowd funding for the Ethereum project started in July 2014, allowing everyone to buy the crypto-currency for Ethereum, Ether (ETH) with bitcoins. As per sources, an amount of $18,439,086 worth of Bitcoins was raised during the crowd funding till the ending date of September 2, 2014. This eventually created 60,102,216 ether tokens. The much awaited live blockchain of Ethereum was launched on 30 July 2015. Ethereum Switzerland GmbH (EthSuisse) and Ethereum Foundation jointly developed the Ethereum software project which was released to the public for Dapp development. The current value of 1 Ether (ETH) is $ 7.39 (as of 07 December 2016, 4:50 pm.)

The Ether (ETH) was a big success in the crypto-currency market with the range of services offered by the Ethereum Project. The market cap of Ether showed a rapid increase and within a short span of time it crossed US $1 billion (by May 2016). While the market leader Bitcoin had a market cap of US $7 billion by that time, Ether started to put on a tight competition with the Bitcoin. Bitcoin struggled to live up to the expectation and was confined more to the currency market while the application developments over the Bitcoin did not taste much success due to the lack of a turing - complete programmable platform. This was the potential opportunity for the Ethereum project to compete with Bitcoin as the Dapp development and smart contract building flourished with the Ethereum platform and many companies and start-ups focused more on Ethereum rather than Bitcoin. Later on, there was a boom in converting the existing applications into the decentralized environment using the Ethereum platform which could disrupt practically every business domain to next level of secure computing.

The Ethereum project is indeed complex and spans over a large array of concepts over various domains like smart contracts, crypto-currency, decentralized applications etc. This could potentially pave way for future blockchain innovations and most of the current mobile and web applications will become upgraded to decentralized platform. In 2014, Vitalik Buterin won the "World Technology Award" for the co-creation and invention of Ethereum.

Ethereum blockchain uses "Patricia Tree" instead of "Merkle Tree" used by the Bitcoin Blockchain. Patricia tree is an evolved form of Merkle tree which stores the data of new transactions, while storing the unchanged data as pointers to the original block location.

Ethereum Releases

According to Buterin's paper 'Opportunities and Challenges for Private and Consortium Blockchains', Ethereum 2.0, the initial scalability release will be on late 2017 and Ethereum 3.0 with 'unlimited' scalability will be released in late 2018.There are four major releases of Ethereum namely Frontier, Homestead, Metropolis and Serenity.

- **Ethereum Frontier:** Frontier was the initial release of the Ethereum network pushed live on 30 July 2015. Frontier is the basic form of the Ethereum network that provides an interface for mining Ether. Before launching the Frontier, a pre-release known as Olympic testnet was launched on May 2015. Frontier was mainly intended to perform Ethereum mining and Ether crypto-currency exchanges such that the participating nodes can start the mining pools to provide consensus for the Dapps being run in the live blockchain network. The rewards will be given to the miners from the transaction fee paid by the sender for each transaction. Frontier was considered as a beta version that allows users to develop, test and upload their Dapps and tools into the Ethereum blockchain.
- **Ethereum Homestead:** The second release of Ethereum platform is Homestead and is the first production release of Ethereum launched in

14 March 2016 at block number 1,150,000. Some major changes in the protocols and network were made in the Homestead while compared to Frontier that could also help in future network upgrades. A few back-ward-incompatible protocol changes were made in Homestead (listed as Ethereum Improvement Proposals in Homestead Documentation) and a hard-fork was also issued for the same (Ethereum Homestead Documentation, 2016).

- **Ethereum Metropolis:** Metropolis will be the next launched with a final official release of a full-fledged user interface for the general users of Ethereum. This will include Mist Browser and a DApp store (like Google Playstore) and several other full-blown projects supported with smart contracts which can leverage the full potential of blockchain net-work. The date is not yet released at the time of writing this book.
- **Ethereum Serenity:**Serenity is the last phase and has one key prin-ciple - to switch the ethereum network from proof of work to proof of stake - essentially reducing the power consumption of the ethereum network. The work may start by early 2017.

The list of currently available Ethereum clients and its description are included in Appendix 1 and the libraries available are included in Appendix 2.

Ethereum Mining

Ethash is the proof of work used in Ethereum 1.0. The Ethereum developers claim that this algorithm is memory hard, which makes it ASIC resistant. Ethash is integrated into the blockchain technology by making the creation of a new block require all members of the network undertake the proof of work based on a set of fixed resources know as DAG (Directed Acyclic Graph). The DAG will be completely updated for every 30000 blocks, a 125-hour window is set called epoch (roughly 5.2 days) and needs some time to gener-ate. As the DAG depends only on the height of the block, it can be generated before the generation of block. If the DAG is not generated, the node has to wait until the process is being committed to produce a block. Consensus is achieved via incentivization for peers to always accept the longest chain of blocks in the blockchain by distribution of a cryptographic token of value: 'ether'. While Ethereum is currently proof of work, it is expected to become proof of stake in its next update, Serenity. Ethereum's development team is more centralized and can therefore can plan and implement POW changes. Changes to the mining algorithm are much harder to implement with Bitcoin and aren't likely to happen. Ethereum's block time is set at 12 seconds per block, while Bitcoin blocks are found on average every 10 minutes. Ethash is the latest version of Dagger-Hashimoto, which is now extensively used in Ethereum network for hashing (Ethereum Homestead Documentation, 2016) The algorithm works as follows:

1. For every block in the blockchain, a seed value exists which is computed by traversing through the block header from genesis block till the current block.
2. A pseudorandom cache (16MB) is computed from the seed which are stored in the light clients.
3. A new dataset (1GB) will be generated from the cache such that the dataset depends only on limited number of items in the cache which exhibits a linear growth. All the nodes and miners will store the copy of the dataset.
4. From the above dataset, random pieces are sliced and hashed together by a process known as mining. The main advantage is that auditing and verification process of this mined data can be carried out with minimum amount of memory. Only the contents of cache is stored as the cache memory can be used to recreate the sliced piece of dataset

After every 30000 blocks, the dataset will be updated and hence the miner's computational power will be used for the reading the data rather than modifying it.

After completing the mining process (PoW) successfully, the miner who mines the winning block will gain:

*   A reward of 5 Ether as the block reward of winning block
*   The gas value spent for the block in terms of Ether equivalent depending on the current gas price.
*   For each uncle being included in the block an extra reward of 1/32 per uncle will be issued to the miner.

Uncles represent the stale blocks, which mean having parents which are ancestors (maximum of 6 preceding blocks) of the current block being included. In order to eliminate the consequence of network lag, the valid uncles are being rewarded while dispersing the mining rewards. Moreover, these valid uncles improve the security as predecessors are maintained effectively. Eventually, the initiators of each transaction will pay for the gas value spent for every transaction inside the winning block being generated by the miner (Ethereum Homestead Documentation, 2016).

Ethereum Transactions

In the Ethereum Project, the "transaction" refers to the signed data package which holds the content to be sent from an EOA (Externally Owned Account) to another account on the blockchain. Every transaction in an Ethereum Blockchain consists of 6 fields namely:

- The recipient of the transaction (either user or smart contract).
- Signature of the sender for identifying and validating the message being sent.
- **VALUE Field:** Specifies the amount of wei to be transferred from the sender to the receiver.
- **DATA Field (Optional):** Holds the message being sent to a contract.
- **STARTGAS Value:** Specifies the maximum number of computational steps that can be carried out by a transaction execution.
- **GASPRICE Value:** Specifies the amount that the sender is willing to pay for gas. One unit of gas corresponds to the execution of one atomic instruction, i.e., a computational step

Ethereum Virtual Machine (EVM)

Ethereum is a programmable blockchain with peer to peer network where every peer stores the same copy of a blockchain database and runs an Ethereum virtual machine to maintain and alter it's state. EVM is a virtual machine designed to be run by all participants in a peer to peer network, it can read and write to a blockchain both executable code and data, Verify digital signatures, and is able to run code in a quasi-Turing complete manner. It will only execute code when it receives a message verified by a digital signature, and the information stored on the blockchain tells it is appropriate to do so. The EVM works in the same way as that of any other virtual machine: it will take any high level programming language designed for writing smart contracts, and can compile it into EVM bytecode that the machine can understand. Ethereum Virtual Machine is typically a huge decentralized computer having millions of accounts. The accounts can be viewed as objects that have the capacity to handle an internal database, run contract code and can communicate with other accounts. The smart contract itself can be considered as an account. Private keys are used for handling the EOAs (Externally Owned Accounts); only the owners of these private keys will have the complete privilege to perform transactions and send ether using EOA (Ethereum Homestead Documentation, 2016).

Ether and Gas

As we have discussed earlier, Ethereum uses its own crypto-currency ether, to execute the contracts over the blockchain. Cost of computation depends on its complexity. Every contract and transaction have a fixed start price used to pay the miner as mining rewards in return for the computational power spend by him. The gas price for any transaction is found by multiplying the number of computations with the current gas price, and thus giving the equation

$$\text{Gas Price}_{\text{Transaction}} = (\text{No. of Computations X Gas Price}_{\text{Current}}) + \text{Start Gas Price}$$

Ethereum project differs from Bitcoin in the fact that the miners will be processing random transactions from the previous blocks and produces hash of the result for the succeeding block. This means that, the smart contracts have the power to carry out any form of computational sequence while the transactions proceeds and can create the chain as per the contractual statement. Moreover, a miner should possess the entire blockchain, so the concept of mining pools does not work same as that of Bitcoin.

Similar to the Bitcoin users, the Ethereum users also have to pay transaction fee to the Ethereum network for performing any transaction over the Ethereum Blockchain. The idea of this transaction fee is to protect the blockchain from the attack of illegitimate users and malicious transactions. Those users possessing enough ether for paying the transaction fee could perform transactions on the blockchain. Similar to bitcoin blockchain, the Ethereum blockchain charges fee for every computation step and data storage. The ether collected by the miners in the Ethereum blockchain will be issued as reward for every valid blocks being mined. These rewards promote more miners to build the blocks of blockchain competitively and to protect the blockchain from attackers (Ethereum Homestead Documentation, 2016).

As we discussed earlier, the notion of Gas in Ethereum blockchain is to incorporate a fixed value for every transaction and computation in the Ethereum network. There are several concepts associated with the Gas like Gas Prices, Gas Cost, Gas Limit, and Gas Fees

- **Gas Cost:** It represents a static cost value for a computation over Ethereum blockchain in terms of Gas. Gas Cost is used in smart contracts to have a control over the computations over time.
- **Gas Price:** It represents the actual cost to be spent as Gas cost in terms of a currency like Ether. Usually the gas price will be floating value to stabilize the value of gas, which means that with the changes in currency values, the gas price also changes to adapt to the value change. The Gas Price is set by the equilibrium price of how much users are willing to spend, and how much processing nodes are willing to accept.
- **Gas Limit:** It specifies the maximum amount of gas that can be used per block. It is depicted as the maximum computational load, volume of transaction, or the block size, and the miners can gradually change the gas limit over a period of time.
- **Gas Fee:** It is the amount of Gas needed to be paid to execute a particular transaction or contract. The miners will get paid with the gas fee based on the computational expenses incurred to build a block.

Working of Ethereum

We will discuss the working of Ethereum as per the present Homestead release. In the Ethereum Project, the underlying blockchain keeps track of the state of each account, and all state transitions happening on the blockchain are transfers of value and information between accounts. The accounts on Ethereum Blockchain can be generally classifies into two categories:

1. Externally Owned Accounts (EOAs): Accounts that are controlled by private key of the users.
2. Contract Accounts: Accounts which are controlled by smart contract code and EOA can activate these contracts.

The major difference between these two accounts is that humans control EOAs – as they own the private keys which give control over an EOA. While, the contract accounts are governed by their "smart contract code". There are certain contract accounts that are "controlled" by humans which are preprogrammed to be controlled by an EOA with a certain address, which is in turn controlled by whoever holds the private keys that control that EOA.

The smart contracts get executed whenever a transaction is being sent to the contract account. Eventually, the users can create new contracts and deploy them in to the blockchain to perform specified tasks.

The EOAs initiate each activity in Ethereum blockchain by starting the concerned transactions. Every time a transaction is received at a contract account, its code gets executed as per the input parameters sent through the transaction. Finally the EVM executes the contract code on each participant in the blockchain network and ends up in creating new block.

The externally controlled account, that are controlled by private keys, possess an ether balance to pay for the transactions to be carried out. They can send transactions even without the associated code. On the other hand, a contract will have an associated code along with the ether balance. The incoming transactions from various external contracts trigger the contract code execution which includes operations of arbitrary complexity. These operations can eventually reflect on the state of the system, can perform storage operations or even invoke other contract codes. Thus the Ethereum can be viewed as a turing complete platform for exploring the potentials to blockchain technology to satisfy the user requirements (Ethereum Homestead Documentation, 2016).

Ethereum Classic

Ethereum Classic is not a new crypto-currency, but instead a split from an existing crypto-currency, Ethereum. Both blockchains are identical in every way up until block 1920000 where the hard-fork to refund The DAO token holders was implemented, meaning that all the balances, wallets, and transactions that happened on Ethereum until the hard-fork are still valid on the Ethereum Classic Blockchain. After the hard-fork, the blockchains were split in two and act individually. The Hard-fork has been a controversial subject, that has split literally split the Ethereum community in two. When the hard-fork was implemented, users that did not agree with it decided not to upgrade their software and to continue mining on the blockchain that did not have this implementation. Since the hard-fork creates an incompatibility between the new and previous versions, the users that decided to remain on the "original" blockchain, have diverged into their own blockchain that is identical to Ethereum's in every way until block 1920000.

The Ethereum Classic is simply a continuation of the basic 'unforked' version of Ethereum Project, called the Ethereum Blockchain. This decentralized platform is free from external interferences and allows tamper-proof transactions controlled through smart contracts. The purpose of Ethereum Classic is to provide a decentralized platform that runs decentralized applications which execute exactly as programmed without any possibility of downtime, censorship, fraud or third party interference.

Ethereum Fork

In the decentralized platform of Ethereum, the ultimate control of the network lies in the hand of the nodes. Even the creators cannot intervene into the network to make changes if needed. In certain critical scenarios (like Ether theft which happened on June 17, 2016) certain decisions have to be taken by the developers, whether to take back power from the miners or to make changes to the immutability of smart contracts. Either of the situations will lead to big conflicts.

This crucial situation forced the developers to introduce a new concept called "fork" which will generally act like a reset button for the Ethereum network. Fork have the ability to cancel transactions and rollback to a stable state. Initial version of fork was "soft fork" which requires large number of miners to agree for the rollback of the network. But this didn't succeed due to security flaws. Later "hard fork" was introduced in which the core Ethereum developers will decide to create a network with new set of rules that are different from the older version. Thereafter the miners can decide whether they have to follow the new network or the older one. The Dapps and smart contracts can also change to the newer version or remain in the older one.

Blockchain can fork into newer versions based on the changing business needs. As of Satoshi's concept of Bitcoin blockchain, the changes made in the fork will have to be adopted by all the beneficiary users/nodes and should stick to the fork from there onwards. Moreover, the new enhancements over the blockchain made by the fork will never affect the previous transactions that are stored immutably over the blockchain. This adds the extra element of robustness and flexibility and leverages an evolutionary model with no baggages.

Deploying Smart Contracts Using Ethereum

Step 1: Start the Ethereum node. Some of the important implementations of Ethereum node are Geth, testrpc, ethersim etc.

Step 2: Compile the smart contract and fetch the binary file for the same. If the smart contract is written in Solidity, use solc compiler to get the binary. Online and offline versions of solc compiler are available for the same.

Step 3: Now deploy the compiled smart contract into the Ethereum network. For this we need the blockchain address of the smart contract and the ABI representation. Deployment needs certain amount of ether (Ethereum blockchain or test network) for connecting with the node's address. Cost of deployment depends on the contract being executed and the gas price needed for execution of various functions in contract.

Step 4: Use JavaScript API of web3.js to access the functions of the contract. This also requires spending of certain amount of ether as specified in smart contract.

Web 3: A platform for Decentralized Apps

Web 3 is actually a back end developed for the decentralized internet service upon the Ethereum platform. According to ethdocs.org, it can represent an internet where core services like DNS and digital identity are decentralized, and where individuals can engage in economic interactions with each other. This sounds quite interesting to have a new Internet built on the invincible blockchain technology with immense potential for developing and deploying Decentralized Applications (Dapps). The dapp projects built on Ethereum will leverage the Ethereum blockchain to build solutions that rely on decentralized consensus to provide new products and services that were not previously possible. As Gavin Wood mentioned, Web 3 will be a "zero-trust interaction system" built on decentralized platform governed by consensus strategy (Ethereum Homestead Documentation, 2016).

REFERENCES

Buterin, V. (2014). *A next-generation smart contract and decentralized application platform*. White Paper.

Ethereum Homestead Documentation. (2016). Retrieved from http://ethdocs.org/en/latest/

Luu, L., Chu, D. H., Olickel, H., Saxena, P., & Hobor, A. (2016, October). Making smart contracts smarter. In *Proceedings of the 2016 ACM SIGSAC Conference on Computer and Communications Security* (pp. 254-269). ACM. doi:10.1145/2976749.2978309

Rosenfeld, M. (2012). *Overview of colored coins*. White paper, bitcoil. co. il.

Sofia. (2016). *Blockchain-Enabled Smart Contracts: Applications and Challenges*. Retrieved from https://letstalkpayments.com/blockchain-enabled-smart-contracts-applications-and-challenges/

Szabo, N. (1997). *The idea of smart contracts*. Nick Szabo's Papers and Concise Tutorials.

Wagner, A. (2016). *Smart Property in Action*. Retrieved from https://bitcoin-magazine.com/articles/smart-property-action-1408049337

Wood, G. (2014). *Ethereum Yellow Paper*. Ethereum.

Chapter 5
Programming the Blockchain

SOLIDITY

Once, the turing-complete Ethereum platform was realized, many programming languages was built on top of it. One of the most prominent and widely used high-level language for developing smart contracts is the Solidity language, whose syntax is similar to that of JavaScript. The Ethereum Virtual Machine (EVM) is used for running the solidity contract codes. Solidity is compiled to byte code that is executable on the EVM. Solidity was initially proposed by Dr. Gavin Wood in August 2014. For the convenience of web developers in developing front end for the smart contracts, Solidity is designed around the ECMAScript (Solidity Tutorials, 2016). Unlike other languages for contract development, Solidity is statically typed and support structures, inheritance, libraries, complex user-defined types and a byte code optimizer. The Application Binary Interface (ABI) which was used for incorporating multiple type-safe functions within a single contract was first introduced in Solidity. Solc is the compiler which is based on C++ libraries is used for compiling the contracts written in solidity. After compiling the contract code with the solc compiler, the byte code can be sent to blockchain network and can call it using the Ethereum web3.js JavaScript API to build web apps that interact

DOI: 10.4018/978-1-5225-2193-8.ch005

with contracts. With Solidity, developers are able to write applications that implement self-enforcing business logic embodied in smart contracts, leaving a non-repudiable and authoritative record of transactions (Solidity, 2016).

SERPENT

Serpent is one of the high-level programming languages used to write smart contracts over Ethereum blockchain. This language is very similar to the Python programming language in its structure and ease of programming (Delmolino, 2015). It is basically intended to be a clean and simple programming language, incorporating most of the efficiency benefits of a low-level language with ease-of-use in programming style. This language has the potential to add exclusive domain-specific features into the contract code.

According to Ethereum Builder's Guide (Ethereum Builder's guide, 2016), the important differences between Serpent and Python are:

- Python numbers have potentially unlimited size, Serpent numbers wrap around 2^{256}. For example, in Serpent the expression $3^{\wedge}(2^{\wedge}254)$ surprisingly evaluates to 1, even though in reality the actual integer is too large to be recorded in its entirety within the universe.
- Serpent has no decimals.
- Serpent has no list comprehensions (expressions like [x**2 for x in my_list]), dictionaries or most other advanced features
- Serpent has no concept of first-class functions. Contracts do have functions, and can call their own functions, but variables (except storage) do not persist across calls.
- Serpent has a concept of persistent storage variables.
- Serpent has an extern statement used to call functions from other contracts.

Forthcoming Programming Approaches / Tools

Mix / Remix

Mix is an IDE (Integrated Development Environment) which aims to facilitate Dapp/Contract creation on top of the Ethereum technology. Mix has been developed using the QML framework and depends on Qt 5.5 (Sfertman, 2016). Mix is a fully integrated development environment which is designed to build and debug smart contracts and their corresponding front ends (Kapplerken, 2016). The Ethereum projects developed in Mix can have smart contracts, html files, javascript files, style files and image files. Mix comes with a project editor to manage the creation and testing of a dapp. It is now officially discontinued and a new version called Remix is launched, which is at its alpha version (Remix, 2016). Emix is now used only for VM debugging. The Mix IDE includes:

- Source code editor for Solidity (contract - backend) and HTML/JS (frontend)
- Solidity source code debugger
- Blockchain editor
- Internal RPC server (allows debugging transactions/calls created from the web3 JavaScript API)
- Dapp/Contract deployment (deploying to test or live chain)

Mist Browser

Mist is the first browser available for the Ethereum blockchain to browse the contracts and Dapps deployed over the blockchain. Mist is simply a user-friendly and powerful tool for running and controlling Dapps without any Command Line Interface (Mist, 2016). It actually provides a face to the blockchain such that the common man can use Dapps and smart contracts just like a regular web application. The Mist browser gives an overall view of the Ethereum blockchain and all the necessary tools required to interact with the blockchain such as the Ether, DAO and the smart contracts (Christoph, 2016).

Truffle

Truffle provides a development environment along with the testing facilities for building Dapps over an Ethereum blockchain. It also provides framework for developing and deploying smart contracts and supports integration of smart contracts with the Dapps (Truffle, 2016). Some of the unique features of Truffle are:

1. Built-in smart contract compilation, linking, deployment and binary management.
2. Automated contract testing with Mocha and Chai.

3. Configurable build pipeline with support for custom build processes.
4. Scriptable deployment & migrations framework
5. Network management for deploying to many public & private networks.
6. Interactive console for direct contract communication
7. Instant rebuilding of assets during development.
8. External script runner that executes scripts within a Truffle environment.
9. Support for JavaScript, SASS, ES6 and JSX built-in.

Meteor

Meteor provides a full stack framework for developing and deploying Dapps over the Ethereum blockchain. It supports real-time web applications over blockchains with embedded smart contracts that can control the working of applications (Tatowicz, 2016). Meteor is the first framework that fully embraced single page app (SPA) development and provided all necessary tools. The major highlights of Metoer are:

1. The development code in the meteor is purely written in Javascript and provides all the tools for SPA. (Templating engine, Model, on-the-fly compiling, bundling)
2. Meteor provides a development environment that supports live reload, CSS injection and support for many pre-compilers (LESS, Coffeescript, etc).
3. Meteor stores all the frontend code as single index.html with one js and css file along with assets, using meteor-build-client.
4. Users can then host the file everywhere or simple run the index.html itself
5. Meteor promotes full reactivity, which make is easy to build a better interface (similar to angualr.js $scope or binding)
6. Meteor supports Minimongo, which provide an interface similar to mongoDB the reactive in-memory database, which can support as a local database.

Embark

Embark is another framework that helps develop and deploy Dapps over the Ethereum Blockchain (Iurimatias, 2016). Major functionalities of Embark are:

1. Embark can automatically deploy smart contracts and can embed it in the JS code.
2. Embark checks for any update in the smart contract, and will automatically redeploy the contracts and the dapp during significant updates
3. Embark can use any build pipeline or tool, including grunt and meteor.
4. Do Test Driven Development with Contracts using Javascript.
5. Can easily deploy and use decentralized systems such as IPFS.
6. Can monitor the deployed contracts.
7. Can handle a variety of chains (e.g testnet, private net, livenet)
8. Can develop complex Dapps that uses multiple contracts and can interact with the decentralized storage systems.

ETHEREUM PRIVATE CHAIN

The programmable blockchain Ethereum allows users to set up private blockchains within the Ethereum network (called testnet) which possess all the features of Ethereum, whereas separated from the Ethereum main network. As most of the developers were new to Ethereum, the testnet was a boon to them. Because, working with the live Ethereum chain having millions of nodes for building a new Ethereum project is really troublesome. For every computation and functions running over the testnet Ether have to spent, which should be owned by the user. Here, we will be discussing the steps involved in creation of testnet with reference to the material from gitbooks.io (Hudson, 2016) and ethdocs.org (Ethdocs, 2016). The testnet will be helpful for the developers to build solutions around the Ethereum platform.

The major components of an Ethereum testnet are:

1. A predefined Genesis File
2. Custom Data Directory
3. Custom NetworkID
4. (Recommended) Disable Node Discovery

The Genesis File

The genesis file is used to define the genesis block (first block) of the blockchain. Generally, the testnet in Ethereum will have a predefined genesis block which is hard coded into the clients with all the essential components. These genesis blocks helps to create customized private blockchains that cater user needs. The consensus algorithm of Ethereum blockchain ensures that no other node will agree with your version of the blockchain unless they have the same genesis block (Ethdocs, 2016).

Sample Customgenesis.json

```
{
    "nonce": "0x0000000000000042",
    "timestamp": "0x0",
    "parentHash": "0x0000000000000000000000000000000000000000000000000000000000000000",
    "extraData": "0x0",
    "gasLimit": "0x8000000",
    "difficulty": "0x400",
    "mixhash": "0x0000000000000000000000000000000000000000000000000000000000000000",
    "coinbase": "0x3333333333333333333333333333333333333333",
    "alloc": {
    }
}
```

Save a file called CustomGenesis.json (or whatever you want to call it). You will reference this when starting your geth node using the flag:

```
--genesis CustomGenesis.json
```

Launching the GETH

After creating the custom genesis block JSON file and created a directory for the blockchain data, type the following command into your console that has access to geth:

```
geth --identity "MyNodeName" --rpc --rpcport "8080" --rpc-
corsdomain "*" --datadir "C:\chains\TestChain1" --port "30303"
--nodiscover --rpcapi "db,eth,net,web3" --networkid 1999 init /
path/to/CustomGenesis.json
```

This command launches the geth and the testnet can be accessed using the geth console. This is the basic operation for setting up the private Ethereum chain. You can find the entire operations over the private chain in (Hudson,2016) and (Ethdocs, 2016).

The testnet from Ethereum was a novel concept which was launched in the early 2015. With the advent of testnet many developers started exploring the potential of the Ethereum blockchain in a much easier and efficient manner. The various launches from Ethereum for building testnet were:

- **Olympic:** It was the pre-release testnet, also referred as Ethereum 0.9. This was launched in early 2015 and was the first public Testnet with the network ID as 0. It was discontinued in July 2015 when the Ethereum launched Morden
- **Frontier:** It was the official 1.0 release, launched as public main network on July 30th, 2015. The Frontier release is the first milestone in the Ethereum project and was intended for use by developers as a beta version. This was the first powerful version of Ethereum and was efficient and capable for building projects over the testnet. Developers began writing smart contracts and decentralized apps to deploy on the live Ethereum network. In addition, miners began to join the Ethereum network to help secure the Ethereum blockchain and earn ether from mining blocks. It has network ID 1
- **Homestead:** It was the first major upgrade (1.1) of the Frontier network in March 2016, but it was not intended to replace Frontier.
- **Morden:** It was the first full release testnet launched parallel to *Frontier* public main network in July 2015. It has network ID 2. It was capable of receiving Homestead updates with the fork update. But, Morden was recently discontinued due to a testnet-only consensus bug between parity and geth.
- **Ropsten:** Has the network ID 3. It was launched in November 2016 and replaces the bugged Morden testnet, and currently runs the latest Homestead branded version of Ethereum. At present all the project working on the Ethereum testnet are running over the ropsten.

The blocks, contracts and the transaction details on the testnet can be viewed at https://testnet.etherscan.io/. by using the appropriate address of the same.

REFERENCES

Christoph. (2016). *Mist*. Retrieved from https://daowiki.atlassian.net/wiki/display/DAO/Mist

Delmolino, K., Arnett, M., Kosba, A., Miller, A., & Shi, E. (2015). *A programmer's guide to ethereum and serpent*. Retrieved from:https://mc2-umd.github.io/ethereumlab/docs/serpent_tutorial.pdf

Ethdocs. (2016). *The Ethereum Network*. Retrieved from http://ethdocs.org/en/latest/network/index.html

Ethereum Builder's Guide. (2016). *Serpent Features*. Retrieved from https://ethereumbuilders.gitbooks.io/guide/content/en/serpent_features.html

Hudson. (2016). *Creating a Private Chain/Testnet*. Retrieved from https://souptacular.gitbooks.io/ethereum-tutorials-and-tips-by-hudson/content/private-chain.html

Iurimatias. (2016). *Embark Framework*. Retrieved from https://github.com/iurimatias/embark-framework/blob/develop/README.md

Kapplerken. (2016). *Your first Dapp*. Retrieved from https://dappsforbeginners.wordpress.com/tutorials/your-first-dapp/

Mist. (2016). *Mist Browser*. Retrieved from https://github.com/ethereum/mist

Remix. (2016). Retrieved from https://github.com/ethereum/remix

Sfertman. (2016). *Mix: The DApp IDE*. Retrieved from https://github.com/ethereum/wiki/wiki/Mix:-The-DApp-IDE

Solidity. (2016). Retrieved from https://solidity.readthedocs.io/en/develop/

Solidity Tutorials. (2016). Retrieved from https://ethereumbuilders.gitbooks.io/guide/content/en/solidity_tutorials.html

Tatowicz, A. (2016). *Dapp using Meteor*. Retrieved from https://github.com/ethereum/wiki/wiki/Dapp-using-Meteor

Truffle. (2016). Retrieved from http://truffle.readthedocs.io/en/latest/

Chapter 6
Current Application Areas

INTRODUCTION

In this chapter we will explore six major domains in which blockchain technology is leveraged for real world problem solving.

FINANCIAL SERVICES

At present, all the banks and financial institutions are maintaining large databases individually which requires high power consumption, manpower and high-end security platforms. With the advent of blockchains, the need for a database can be completely eliminated and every bank could make transaction on a single chain which could even replace the physical existence of a bank. It can drastically reduce the settlement time between banks and clearing houses from several banking days down to a number of minutes, or even seconds with literally zero possibility for double –spend or fake transaction. Unlike bitcoin blockchain which was anonymous and permission-less, blockchains for financial services would be permissioned and private with potential for permission-less versions also. In future, the banks can cover the clients globally without the need of an office at every location but virtually through the

DOI: 10.4018/978-1-5225-2193-8.ch006

blockchain network. This will reduce the operational cost, transaction fee and need of employees and makes the business highly profitable. Blockchain also explores the potential for linking with other business paradigms which could create opportunity for improving the business models of financial institutions (Hyperledger, 2016). Financial institutions now trust in smart contracts as a practical solution to cut overhead costs and to speed up trading and settlement. Major banks like Citi and J.P. Morgan, along with clearinghouses like the Depository Trust & Clearing Corporation, are in the process of building and testing smart contracts to trade credit default swaps.

An example of bank creating an open access platform for handling currency is LHV (an Estonian Bank). LHV is testing blockchain with EUR 100, 000 worth of 'cryptographically protected' receivables claims against the bank. LHV make use of one of the prominent open source protocol over Bitcoin Blockchain, the "colored coins" for creating CUBER (Cryptographic Universal Blockchain Entered Receivables). CUBER represents a novel certificate of deposit which can be used as a building block for developing wide range of financial products and services. This will allow the customers to make free person-to-person fiat currency payments using blockchain. LHV have future plans to promote financial innovation through small-scale software developers, as well as encourages start-ups and crypto-currency exchanges to leverage to potential of this platform (Higgins, 2016).

In general, blockchain-based value transfer and financial systems have some major technical benefits when compared to traditional systems. The private individuals can enjoy more privacy, security and hassle-free monitoring and control over their financial assets at a reasonable cost. For major businesses, blockchain technology could cut the processing fees, enable faster global payment, and reduces the risk of chargeback fraud drastically.

Recently, the Santander Bank - U.K. has introduced a pilot app built on blockchain technology for international payments. This app was developed by Ripple, which can connect to Apple Pay, where the users can perform secure transactions through TouchID. Santander is the first bank in U.K. to adopt blockchain technology for payments and aims at revolutionizing the entire banking operation, infrastructure and systems which this approach (Prisco, 2016a).

Nano-Payments

Nano-payments are tiny payments for a trivial service over blockchains for value – based transfer systems. This is highly useful for very small transactions involving fractions of a currency. For nano-payments, security is associated with the token or means of payment. In the traditional payment systems, there are fixed transaction charges, technological constraints and other overheads which made such transactions more or less unfeasible on a large scale (Mattila, 2016).

PUBLIC NOTARY SYSTEM

The notion of public notary system was first released by Bitnation which calls itself a "governance 2.0" service. Bitnation is a blockchain-powered virtual-nation platform which leverages the potential of bitcoin blockchain technology to provide all the traditional governmental services in the distributed environment. Validating identities, notarization and dispute settlement were some of the major services initially provided by Bitnation (Bitnation, 2016).

Bitnation collaborated with the Estonian government on December 01, 2015 to offer public notary services to Estonian e-Residents. The citizens are provided with a Public Key Infrastructure (PKI) card with which they can get access to over 1000 governmental services electronically. The PKI card possesses a 4-digit pin for authorizing digital signatures of e-documents which are legal throughout the European Union. With the PKI card, Estonian e-Residents from all over the world can now officially notarize birth certificates, marriage arrangements, testaments, business contracts, land titles, or any other such documents through Bitnation's service. The e-residency system also offers an opportunity for Estonian citizens to run businesses or companies online and can provide services globally.

In the recent past, Bitnation introduced the refugee emergency response program to deal with the refugee crisis in the European Union. This project includes providing refugees with authenticated identification documents that can help in reuniting families, debit cards that are directly linked to accounts of donated cryptocurrency, and other such immediate firsthand services (Prisco, 2016b).

The digital document provenance is the capability of any notary system to prove that the document existed in the specified format at a certain instant of time. This can be done by using the address of the document generated from the cryptographic hash value of the same document. Crypto Public Notary created by Alex Sherbuck is a free notary service running over the bitcoin blockchain for providing digital provenance of documents.

DIGITAL ASSETS AND STOCK

Blockchain based distributed public ledger could disrupt the current asset transfer and real estate market with improved transparency, efficiency and security in how records are transmitted, recorded and stored. This could revolutionize the industry my automating the major functions such as payment, escrow, and title using smart contracts. Many experts suggest that implementation of blockchain has the potential to reduce fraud, increase privacy, speed up transactions, and open up international markets.

Currently, the amount of digital assets over the Internet is increasing at a faster pace. But, most of these digital assets face the potential challenges of privacy, security, counterfeiting etc. which turns out to be the major hindrances in dealing these assets. With the immutable public ledgers providing privacy and security, blockchains can provide a safe storage facility for the highly valuable digital assets, bonds, keys and stocks. "Coloredcoins" provide an open-source protocol for creating digital assets over the bitcoin blockchain. Stocks are one of the major digital assets that can be handled over the blockchains (Rosenfeld, 2012). Various companies can use Coloredcoins to issue shares of their companies instead of using the conventional stock exchanges like NASDAQ and NYSE (Castillo, 2016). The shares can be traded without any middleman or brockerage firms. The NYSE has invested in blockchain provider Coinbase in 2015 and ASX (Australian Securities Exchange) has partnered with Digital Assets Holdings for designing blockchain solutions for stock markets. NASDAQ has already launched blockchain-based solution 'LINQ' for trading private ownership shares digitally. LINQ follows the concept of distributed ledger to make entry for all the transactions carried out at NASDAQ. This project is still in infancy and NASDAQ expects to release the full-blown version of LINQ in the coming future.

IDENTITY SERVICES

One of the most promising areas where Blockchain technology found its relevance is the identity services. Identification and reputation management services are made possible by the immutable public ledger mechanism of the blockchains. Blockchain based identity services also eliminated the need for intermediaries for verification and validation by using the consensus protocols (Mattila, 2016).

Blockchain technology can revolutionize the existing digital identity services in two main aspects. Firstly, it eliminated the need for a trusted third party and related protocols, thus eliminating the expenses incurred by them. It also minimizes the unnecessary and time consuming channels of routine validations which is of no use.

Secondly, the digital identities over the distributed public ledger are more ubiquitous in that can be easily integrated to any decentralized service upon the agreement of concerned stakeholders with the help of smart contracts. Thus the identities of completely unknown entities can be made trustworthy and the reputation can also be improved (Mattila, 2016). One of the emerging blockchain based identity service is the Citizen ID concept by The Republic of Estonia with the help of Bitnation to provide unique ID and digital key to every citizen of the nation. We have already mentioned the work of Bitnation in Public notary system in the previous section. The identity service through the e-Residents programme forms the foundation of public notary system. Onename is another startup company which focuses on developing blockchain based identities that can be used as credential at various online websites.

VOTING SYSTEMS

As Stalin said, "It doesn't matter who votes, but who counts the votes". Same is the case with online voting scenario also. To uphold the virtue of impartiality and neutrality are the basic requirements on any voting mechanism. There was always a question of doubt over the pattern of election and voting results due to human intervention at several points which was unavoidable in the current scenario. Most of the voting systems are centralized in nature and the source code, database and output pattern of these systems are purely defined by the developers. Blockchain technology could introduce a drastic change in this pattern. An open-source and independently verifiable ballot system improves the trust of the voters. For a fair election process, the system supporting the ballot should be tamper-proof and auditable. Moreover, it should be anonymous and unintermediated such that the chance for an inappropriate vote is zero (Mattila, 2016).

Most of the Blockchain based voting systems mimic the logic of crytocurrency blockchains. Only difference is that, instead of coins, the votes will be send as transaction obeying some consensus to the public ledger. With the fact that the immutable blockchain ledger is public and anonymous, the identity of the voters can be kept secret whereas the voting outcome can be made public without any tampering. This eliminates the possibility of any fudging or illegal votes and uphold the voting right of every citizen for a fair cause.

'FollowMyVote' is the first open-source online voting protocol built over the blockchain technology. Votosocial.org introduced a proof of concept of an e-voting solution built using the colored coins protocol on the bitcoin blockchain to perform online voting over blockchain platform.

SUPPLY CHAIN

Supply chains include hundreds of transaction starting from the procurement of raw materials through production and finally selling the end-product to customers. The blockchains can enhance the security of transaction and can efficiently maintain book-keeping eliminating the chances of fraud. One of the biggest players in the supply chain, the middleman can be completely avoided by the blockchains as the public ledgers can take over their role and can connect all the concerned stakeholders smoothly. Supply chains will be more transparent and the auditing will be simplified. Smart contracts can be incorporated to control the smooth processing and transportation of goods and will be highly useful in handling volatile and perishable goods. This can significantly reduce transaction costs, human errors and delivery delays.

IBM and Walmart are jointly developing blockchain powered supply chain by using the concept of Hyperledger project. They developed this project initially for the pork supply in China. Here, the quality of meat can be ensured right from the farm to stores through the transaction history stored in IBM's private blockchain. Blockchain improves traceability and transparency throughout the supply chain and can initiate product recall if it gets damaged in the transit. The point of failure and remedial measures can be initiated quickly with the blockchains so that the customers will receive quality goods. This was a tiresome job in the existing supply chain. Eventually, the product quality and customer loyalty can be improved so as to overcome the existing competitors in the traditional supply chain.

PwC is also testing on potential of blockchains on supply chain in areas like customs clearance, trade finance, chain of custody, digital document trade etc. PwC aims at developing a transparent supply chain with easier authentication of shipments through blockchain technology.

Everledger is a blockchain-based company which focuses on tracking precious diamonds using laser-inscribed serial numbers, digital thumbprints of attributes, and a distributed public ledger. They keep track of diamonds right from the mine through various processing steps and finally to the buyers in distributed public ledger. This allows easier verification of quality and authenticity of the product and will eliminate the chances of fraud (Kastelein, 2016).

REFERENCES

Bitnation. (2016). *Public Notary System: Bitnation*. Retrieved from https://bitnation.co/notary/

Castillo, M. (2016). *Nasdaq Opens Blockchain Services to Global Exchange Partners*. Retrieved from http://www.coindesk.com/nasdaqs-blockchain-services-global-exchange/

Higgins, S. (2016). *LHV Bank Develops Wallet App Built on Bitcoin's Blockchain*. Retrieved from http://www.coindesk.com/lhv-bank-backs-wallet-app-built-on-bitcoins-blockchain/

Hyperledger. (2016). *Blockchain rewires financial markets: Trailblazers take the lead*. IBM Institute for Business Value.

Kastelein, R. (2016). *Everledger Rolls Out Blockchain Technology to Digitally Certify Kimberley Diamonds*. Retrieved from http://www.the-blockchain.com/2016/09/20/everledger-rolls-out-blockchain-technology-to-digitally-certify-kimberley-diamonds/

Mattila, J. (2016). *The Blockchain Phenomenon–The Disruptive Potential of Distributed Consensus Architectures (No. 38)*. The Research Institute of the Finnish Economy.

Prisco, G. (2016a). *Santander Becomes First U.K. Bank to Introduce Blockchain Technology for International Payments*. Retrieved from https://bitcoinmagazine.com/articles/santander-becomes-first-u-k-bank-to-introduce-blockchain-technology-for-international-payments-1464795902

Prisco, G. (2016b). *Bitnation Launches World's First Blockchain-Based Virtual Nation Constitution*. Retrieved from https://bitcoinmagazine.com/articles/bitnation-launches-world-s-first-blockchain-based-virtual-nation-constitution-1455895473

Rosenfeld, M. (2012). *Overview of colored coins*. White paper, bitcoil. co. il.

Chapter 7
Emerging Opportunities with Blockchain

INTRODUCTION

In this chapter, we primarily explore the technological and business areas that can have a disruption with the application of blockchains. We also discuss a few novel business opportunities that could get created with this new technology.

DECENTRALIZED IoT

The Internet of Things (IoT), cloud and blockchain are three massive tech trends that could combine to create an entirely new method of data process known as IoT-based computation. This development looks at the 'art of the possible' and this new way of thinking could provide powerful ways for a business to run autonomously (Crosby, 2015).

As per Gartner estimations 5.5 million new 'things' get connected to the internet every day populating the IoT world rapidly. Technology analyst also forecast a huge growth in the number of connected things from nearly 4.9 billion devices at the end of 2015 to 20.8 billion by 2020.

DOI: 10.4018/978-1-5225-2193-8.ch007

A conventional, centralized approach would be an expensive undertaking in terms of time, personnel, infrastructure, logistics, and money. Blockchain technology provides an alternative that allows any single participant to essentially "outsource" the management, communications and scalable infrastructure problems to the peer-to-peer network that maintains the blockchain. Instead of using a central server, a distributed public ledger will be maintained to store the transaction records of "things" and every node will possess a copy of this immutable public ledger.

The "scalability" feature of blockchain can be utilized to accommodate 'things' in the IoT world. The number of IoT devices is expected to increase into multiple billions and developing centralized control to accommodate these enormous numbers of things to the system will not be viable, both economically and technically. As mentioned by Crosby, It should be noted that the use of blockchains to support IoT computing does not magically eliminate the cost of infrastructure or communications. In the end, the bits have to get to where the bits have to get to, and somebody, somewhere, is going to have to pay to make that happen; nothing is free (Crosby, 2015).

Blockchain technology provides the ability to redistribute costs across all of the participants of the peer-to-peer network, and give each peer an economic motivation to provide their (small) part of the infrastructure needed to enable the greater good. This reduces the burden on any individual peer, while allowing them to leverage the resources of all. The cost to add a message to the chain is a small "transaction fee," so a broadcast type message could be added to the blockchain, and be received by literally a billion or more IoT devices for very little relative direct cost to the sender; this is not possible with a centralized approach. In the coming future, the blockchain powered IoT devices will find its application in smart appliances, precision farming sensors, self-driving vehicles, supply chain monitoring sensors etc.

IBM and Samsung introduced a Proof-of Concept of Blockchain powered IoT system called ADEPT, in which they demonstrated a self-sufficient washing machine over decentralized IoT (Panikkar, 2014). We will discuss more details about ADEPT in the coming sections.

Filament, a blockchain-based startup had developed IoT-powered sensors called "Taps" for establishing low power autonomous mesh networks mainly focusing on data and asset management.

Chain of Things (CoT) is a consortium which is focused on exploring the potential of Blockchain-based Decentralized IoT and the security issues in the IoT sector. As per the sources, they are focusing on developing IoT hardware components backed with blockchains to provide solutions to IoT security.

IBM developed Watson IoT platform that supports IoT devices to perform transactions over the private blockchain network. This allows businesses to track every transaction over the IBM's tamper-proof public ledger and thus prevents disputes over the transactions

Decentralized Autonomous Organizations (DAO)

Decentralized Autonomous Organization (DAO) is simply a program code that runs over the peer-to-peer network and works according to the specified governance rules and guidelines. Generally, the DAO's work autonomously and accomplish task without any human intervention. With the advent of the programmable blockchain platform, Ethereum, the organization framework for the DAO's can be embedded as self-executing smart contracts that can define the entire operations of the organization. Every function of the DAO is preprogrammed into that code. Since the code runs on the blockchain, it runs on thousands of computers at the same time, making it very powerful and stable. Moreover, the code of a DAO can only be altered if 51% of the members of the DAO agree with the proposed new code. No other conditions can alter the DAO's code, thus making it truly autonomous. The DAO's code is actually the business logic built over smart contracts which execute transactions that are triggered by predefined conditions. The results of these transactions get written onto the blockchain. Ether is used as fuel for running transactions over DAO (Swan, 2015).

The contract code by itself is decentralized and runs on thousands of nodes all over the world at the same time. Another decentralized characteristic is that anyone can participate in a DAO by acquiring tokens. Tokens are shares in a DAO and can be acquired, mostly in exchange for money. With tokens you can take part, collaborate, propose, rate and vote to name a few possible activities. If you want out, you can sell your tokens at the current market price, via an exchange. This open participation makes the DAO decentralized.

ADePT: A Prototype Implementation of a DAO

IBM introduced the ADePT (Autonomous Decentralized Peer-To-Peer Telemetry) platform, which is built around the idea of decentralization to provide security and scalability to IoT. The ADePT concept uses blockchain technology to provide the backbone of the system, utilizing a mix of peer-to-peer protocols to get secure and fault tolerant transactions. In ADePT, the blockchain is seen as a way for devices to understand what other devices do, and the instructions and permissions different users have around these devices. In practice this can mean tracking relationships between a user and a device, and even between two devices, with the consent of the user. The initial ADePT PoC consisted of three main use-cases: an automated door lock, a smart washer and a wearable. IBM and Samsung jointly developed the PoC for automated washer by reconfiguring the Samsung W9000 washing machine to work within the ADePT platform. This washer has the capability to place order to detergent supplier whenever it needs supplies. Based on the contract code, it can also make automated payments for the orders it had placed. With a connected mobile application, the washer can share the details of purchase and operation to the owner (Panikkar, 2015).

In order to realize the ADePT concept, IBM and Samsung chose three protocols:

- Ethereum, in order to allow devices to understand contracts and capabilities (this is where blockchain technology comes into play);
- Telehash, a private messaging protocol used to share information among two or more devices;
- Bit Torrent, a file sharing protocol used to move data around also in case of discontinuous and unreliable connections.

DECENTRALIZED SOCIAL NETWORKS

Social networking websites like Facebook, YouTube, Twitter etc is contributing more as a sales driver than a communication platform. Most of the online shopping platforms are supported by the social networking sites in promoting their products. The novel idea of Decentralized Social Networks (DSN) over blockchains had kick started into this arena such that the users will get paid for the value they generated (Kate, 2016). Here the user's contribution towards the social networks will be traced and a rewarding mechanism will be set up to acknowledge their contributions. With the reward mechanism and the privacy and security ensured by the blockchains, this revolutionary concept will definitely attract more users to the DSN platform. Till date, the DSN is in the very early stage of development and certain companies like DECENT, Datt, AKASHA, Diaspora, Synereo etc are working on its development. DECENT is an open-source decentralized content distribution platform that uses the blockchain technology to ensure privacy and security (Bogdan, 2016).

DECENTRALIZED CLOUD STORAGE

The present cloud storage systems spend huge amount of money to develop systems that ensure account privacy and data security. Also, most of the present cloud storage systems are centralized and the credibility of the service provider will be an important challenge for the storage. With the immutable public ledger mechanism of blockchain technology, the storage systems for cloud can be completely converted into the decentralized platform. This allows greater availability of resources as every node can have the copy of the ledger. Also the consensus approach and trust-free paradigm of the blockchain ensures improved security and monitoring to the service utilization. The micropayment mechanism can ensure better billing mechanism for usage of cloud storage. In a scenario when there is large amount of data, there is no need to store all the data into the blockchain, but rather we store only the file metadata. Eventually, the blockchain contains the hash, the network locations of files being stored, and the corresponding merkle roots. Usually, the data will be inserted into the blockchain through normal transactions with an extra metadata. The traditional cloud storage systems will be replaced by distributed cloud storage systems, where the data will be available across a number of connected systems. Distributed storage systems will reduce the down-time and ensures high availability of data.

For example, Storj is a blockchain based, end-to-end encrypted, distributed object storage mechanism where data is shredded and stored across a collection of distributed computers. Only the user with valid key can access the data. Storj runs on the users' machines and the users will be rewarded with tokens (StorjcoinX) for providing the disk space for storage (Wilkinson et al., 2014).

The music industry is now leveraging the potential of blockchain technology for publishing content and monetizing the usage with micropayments. With the public ledger system, the files can be published in a censorship-resistant manner and discrepancies over the ownership can be avoided by the sequential time-stamping of blockchains. The ownership rights and copyright agreements will be also published in the public ledger such that anyone can easily verify it (O'Dair, 2016).

ROLE OF SMART CONTRACTS IN POLICY MAKING

We have already discussed the potential of self-executing smart contracts over blockchains and the role of smart properties in adding values to the businesses. Similar to the way in which Internet made disruptive revolution in the transaction processing and communication, the smart contracts could be significantly important in policy making process as the agreements and norms of any process can be digitalized to control every transaction happening over the blockchain network. In other words, smart contracts will act as a virtual controller that monitor and direct each transaction to the restrictions mandated in the contract statement. Smart contracts provide maximum accuracy to transactions with very less risks to the stakeholders (Pilkington, 2016).

Hedgy is a startup which focuses on developing smart contracts working over distributed public ledgers. Hedgy has already launched certain usecase aimed at bitcoin miners. Mirror is another smart contract development community that focuses on developing contracts for peer-to-peer trading and financial services. Blockstream is another company which develops smart contracts mainly for financial services. They also focus on the potential of side-chain and cross-chain compatibility over blockchains that can communicate across different blockchains.

HYPERLEDGER PROJECT

Hyperledger is a novel approach of cross-industry blockchain technology developed through an open-source collaborative effort with entities from banking, IoT, manufacturing, finance, supply chain and technology. This project is hosted as a collaborative project under Linux Foundation. The aim of this project is to help software engineers to develop industry-specific and enterprise-grade open-source applications over the public ledger system. Hyperledger works over a permissioned network that can process both public and private transactions without the support of any crypto-currency. According to hyperledger.org, this project ensures interoperability, transparency, longevity and support for the blockchains to be used as a mainstream commercial software development resource (IBM Blockchain, 2016).

DIGITAL CERTIFICATES AND ACADEMIC RECORDS

Today when you get a credential from an institution, you receive a piece of paper, but ultimately anybody who wants to verify that credential goes back to the source.. Learners may obtain certificates on various courses from different universities at different times. This makes the verification process time consuming and extremely difficult. Also obsolete courses offered by institutions and new models of higher education are complicating the verification process

The use of blockchain technology will make the whole process of maintaining records more cost efficient, transparent and secure. In this approach, a learner-centered transcript is stored in a distributed ledger to record transactions. A transcript is the record of what a student has accomplished at a university. The document is managed and controlled by the institution, not the student.

Crating and Issuing a digital certificate is relatively simple with blockchain: a digital file is created which contains some basic information such as the learner name, course name, year of graduation, name of the university, an issue date, etc. Then the contents of the certificate are signed using a private key to which only the institution has access, and will append that signature to the certificate itself. Next, a hash is created which can be used to verify that nobody has tampered with the content of the certificate. Finally private key is used again to create a record on the blockchain which means that a certain certificate is issued to a learner on a certain date. This makes it possible to verify who a certificate was issued to, by whom, and validate the content of the certificate itself.

In addition to efficiency and security, storing academic records on the blockchain technology will enable students to access their credentials and certificates at anytime from anywhere in the world without having to worry about losing the certificates or having to get it reissued from their universities. These digital certificates are durable, time-stamped, transparent and decentralized. Maintaining educational records on blockchain will not only allow students to readily access their academic records as mentioned earlier, but it will also allow the prospective employers to access the same for employment purposes. A unified distributed ledger with details of all students on a single blockchain will make it a one-stop shop for students, employers, and institutions to access, share and verify the credentials based on the type of permission they have. This will also prevent counterfeiting and fraud of educational degrees while bringing the educational system up to speed with current technologies (Prisco, 2016a).

For example, The University of Nicosia in Cyprus is one of the early adopters of blockchain technology for maintaining student records. The MIT Media Lab began issuing digital certificates to the participants in its Director's Fellows program.

DECENTRALIZED MARKETS

Decentralized market is path-breaking innovation that helps people to buy/sell goods directly with others without the involvement of any trading institutions. This will disrupt the present e-commerce markets and the business giants like Amazon, ebay, flipkart etc. will have be dethroned from the online trade through decentralized markets. With person-to-person trade, the prices will be much low as the overheads for warehousing and other handling processes will get eliminated.

OpenBazaar provides a decentralized marketplace where goods can be purchased using Bitcoins. There is no transaction fee or restrictions in the OpenBazaar and there is no governing body or controlling authorities. Anybody can sell any product through this peer-to-peer network by downloading the application.

Slock.it is another group which focuses on the possibilities of blockchain to allow persons to seel, buy or rent properties over the peer-to-peer network without any intermediaries. Slock.it has partnered with Airbnb for renting houses and apartments through pay-per-use facility controlled by smart access facilities (Prisco, 2016b). Here anybody can rent the unused spaces of office or house to anyone across the world through a smart contract which controls the terms of use, payments and other procedures.

DECENTRALIZED RIDE SHARING PLATFORMS

The online centralized ride sharing applications like Uber are now facing tough competition from the decentralized ride sharing applications running over blockchains. The concept of smart transport systems are now being built over blockchains to ensure fair billing, passenger authentication, vehicle statistics reporting etc. The immutable data store concept can maintain proper transaction history and the smart contracts could ensure fair usage policies. Smart contract allows negotiation of fare, micropayments, proper driver incentives and distributing unused ride slots at lower fares. In future self-driving cars can also adopt this decentralized ride sharing platforms for better connectivity.

La'Zooz is an online decentralized ride sharing platform built over block-chains. It uses its own token known as "Zooz" to pay rewards to users and drivers. Rather than focusing on adding more vehicles on street, La'Zooz aims at efficiently utilizing the existing infrastructure properly. The distributed public ledger technology is being utilized here to synchronize all the trans-actions happening over the ride sharing. With the complete decentralization anybody can join La'Zooz and no government or authorities have any form of control over this business model (Lazooz, 2016).

Arcade City is another blockchain based ride sharing and car hiring plat-form which provides complete freedom for the providers/drivers to set fare and negotiate rides for the customers. Arcade city is actually a global com-munity of decentralized peer-to-peer service providers and consumers which focuses on Ethereum blockchain applications. It is inspired from Openbazaar, a decentralized market platform based on bitcoin blockchain. Arcade city now plans to develop home rental and peer-to-peer delivery platforms.

Healthcare

Healthcare is one of the prime areas where privacy and accuracy of input data needs high attention. The immutable public ledger mechanism of blockchains helps to achieve security and privacy of patient data and medical records. Also, the volume of data to be handled in the healthcare sector increases ex-ponentially over years making it difficult to handle in centralized databases. Blockchains can efficiently connect to various monitoring devices to fetch medical data and can run smart contracts over it to infer conclusions to be stored immutably.

Tierion is the first company to start blockchain based healthcare project by partnering with Philips blockchain lab. They collect day-to-day medical records and feedback from patients and store in immutably over blockchains to help practitioners to provide better medical care and personal attention. Philips developed and app-based ultrasound system called "Lumify" through which user can connect to a transducer and can fetch high-quality ultrasound images without going to a medical lab (Tieron, 2016). The system generates transaction receipts for every medical activity so that the doctors and patients can know the state of the disease and treatment statistics. In future, the medical insurance companies will also be incorporated into the blockchain such that the financial assistance and payments can be carried out through live blockchains without any delay.

Decentralized Power Grid

Nowadays, more and more households are getting equipped to generate renewable energy from solar, wind, bio-gas and other sources. In this scenario, these households can sell the power thus generated to power management corporations through a centralized grid. The transmission through centralized grid causes power loss due to heat dissipation and storage requires heavy expenditure. Moreover, the corporate entities owning the grids will pay very less amount for the power taken from the household. The central power grids faced the problem of massive power outages due to grid failures. These issues gave rise to the notion of a decentralized power grid, where the household can buy/sell power to peers/neighbors without any third-party grid and can gain better income. Decentralized grids can save large amount of power which lost as heat during transmission from centralized grid. Eventually, this provides resilience to massive power outages due to central grid failure.

With the rise of IoT powered smart devices, the devices are becoming self-sufficient and are able to communicate with each other. These devices are even capable of generating and trading power over the grid. By leveraging the potential of decentralized power grids, every device in the grid can buy and sell power and generate income for their survival. The blockchain technology has the potential to provide a peer-to-peer decentralized grid to connect smart devices across the world. With the immutable transactions over the public ledger, the consumption, billing and payment for the power used/generated will be more efficient (Tapscott, 2016).

LO3 energy (New York) and Siemens partnered together to develop blockchain based micro-grid called Brooklyn, which can be used a distributed energy trading platform. This enables blockchain-based local energy trade among the households with solar PV installations through a smart contract developed over Ethereum platform.

Clinical Trials

Clinical trials involve developing new drugs and compounds that are effective for human beings without much side-effect. The average cost of development of a drug lies in the range of 700 million to 1.5 Billion US dollars and takes a time span of 15 – 20 years. In many situations, the researchers will not be able to fetch good results even after spending this huge amount of money and time. There are chances that the organizations may force the researchers to fudge the data and experiment process to get better results at low cost to gain maximum profit. Eventually, these kinds of malpractices may cause serious harm to humans when the drugs are released in the market. Also, the present clinical trials the government organizations cannot monitor and audit every step in clinical trials as most of the confidential data lies in the centralized database of the research institutes. In 2015, Springer had withdrawn 64 articles and BioMed Central had withdrawn 43 articles due to the fraudulent findings in medical trail data. This created a need for a censorship-resistant medical trial monitoring system which can be viewed publicly across the concerned stakeholders and thus the blockchain technology was introduced into the clinical trial process.

Blockchain-based decentralized public ledgers has evolved as an excellent data store for handling every process in the clinical trials. They can distribute data across various participating entities of the trial and can also establish consensus strategy for critical processes. Smart contracts can be deployed over the blockchain to ensure that every process follows the necessary protocols of the trails. This can also connect the electronic monitoring devices directly to the blockchains and reduce human interventions which in turn reduce the chances of malpractices. The immutable public ledger eliminates the chance of any data fudging and the regulatory boards and governments can have the clear picture of the clinical trials.

The blockchains also reduce the cost of auditing as the distributed ledgers are public and works over the consensus. This also speeds up the trials with the protocols specified in the smart contracts. Currently, clinicians are working on a pilot project on exploring the potential of blockchains in clinical trials with the use-case of research on cardiovascular diabetes and ethanol.

Distributed Artificial Intelligence Platforms

Artificial Intelligence (AI) is always a hot topic of research among the enthusiasts. Recently, the AI researchers are focusing on the potential of developing a distributed artificial intelligence platforms that has the potential to generate distributed solutions for complex problems.

Neureal is a project that aims at developing a blockchain-powered peer-to-peer open-source AI computing capability that can be put into production for modeling the world. This project uses a distributed artificial intelligence crypto-currency protocol that can efficiently utilize the idle computing power to users for obtaining solutions of AI problems. This can utilized for future prediction, big data analysis, question-answer models and evaluating theories for all possible domains (Redman, 2015).

Here, every node in the network can run different AI algorithms to make predictions on the data inputs coming to the system. Any individual can add a node to the AI network with concerned algorithm for proposing solution. The crypto-currency protocol of the Neureal will reward the accurate predictions and will eventually lead to an evolutionary development towards higher degrees of accuracy for prediction. In the peer-to-peer network the nodes share predictions with each other to improve analytics. Eventually, these nodes can form hierarchical structures and can utilize the potential of deep learning into it.

Blockchain as a Service

Technology giants are now exploring on the possibility of Blockchain as a Service to extent its potential to more business domains. Microsoft and ConsenSys entered a partnership to create Ethereum Blockchain as a Service (EBaaS) on Microsoft Azure which aims at a cloud-based blockchain developer environment. Their focus is mainly aimed at the scope of distributed public ledger for developers and clients. Clients can create private, public or consortium based blockchains by using this service (Shieber, 2015).

IBM has also announced Blockchain-As-A-Service to developers by leveraging the potential of the distributed ledger technology. IBM also uses its Bluemix platform for designing and deploying applications over blockchains that could use the cloud services of the company. The high performance mainframe computers called IBM z servers are used to deploy the consensus algorithm for various business use-cases. IBM supports modularity with the pluggable architecture of the IBM's code such that the software modules and smart contracts can be customized according to the client needs.

ESCROW SERVICE

Traditionally, escrow services provided a financial agreement where a neutral intermediary performed transactions for the various parties involved in the agreement. As we have already discussed about the elimination of middle-man by the blockchains, the escrow services can also be disrupted by the blockchains. The escrow services over the blockchains work on the basis of private/public keys to control the transaction specified in the agreement. These multi-signature concepts over the immutable public ledger provide transparency for the transactions and avoid the chances of fraud. This can also avoid the overhead of middleman, dispute settlements and time delay of transactions. Third Key Solutions is a start-up company that offers escrow services based on the bitcoin operations.

Prediction Markets

Prediction markets are exchange-traded markets which are established for trading the outcome of events. These markets allow users to buy and sell shares based on probability of each event calculated from the opinion of all the stake-holders. The current predication markets are centralized and easily shut down if the stake-holders withdraw. Moreover, every event occurring in the centralized prediction market has to be reported. This is generally done by an individual, which has chances for errors, fraud and fudging. The decentral-ized predication markets built over blockchains could disrupt the conventional markets with reputation-based predication from all the stakeholders. Augur and Gnosis are some of the upcoming decentralized prediction markets which could replace the current prediction markets like PredictIt (Augur, 2016).

Micro-Insurance

Nowadays the notion of ownership of an asset is becoming fluid among the younger generation, as they tend to believe more in sharing economy. Rather than purchasing a product/service by spending a lump sum amount, people now choose to lend the product/service whenever they need it. The lender and borrower always need a trusted third party for maintaining the contract for lending. This process of lending can be controlled through a micro-insurance which ensures payments to lender and guarantees compensation in case of any loss/damage. This creates a potential business opportunity for blockchains to develop a secure platform for lending, without the need of a trusted-third party. Lendberbot is a blockchain-based micro-insurance proof of concept developed by Stratumn, Deloitte and Lemonway that uses a simple chat-bot for ensuring the terms of contract (Stratumn, 2016).

Lenderbot utilizes Facebook messenger as chat-bot through which the lender and borrower can agree on the contract of lending. This mainly aims at insuring high-valued products/ services offered through lending contracts. Every transaction through the Lenderbot are cryptographically-connected to each other and stored in the public ledger of Blockchain such that the transaction are visible to every party involved in lending.

Governance

The UK Government Digital Service is developing a digital platform over the distributed public ledger system for the government to deliver its services to the citizens. This project is intended to make the delivery of services more personal, fast and efficient. Smart contracts will be embedded over the distributed ledgers to incorporate all the protocols of governance with proper legal validities (Walport, 2016). As per the report of the UK Government Chief Scientific Adviser, this project aims at improving the transparency and traceability of the government policies and rules, reduces operational costs, improves security, reduces tax frauds and creates opportunities for economic growth. In future, this will also revolutionize the capital markets, KYC (Know Your Customer) registry, law and legal trails, reconciliations and settlements and ultimately position UK as a global leader.

Food Supply Chain

IBM, Walmart and Tsinghua University (China) are developing a collaborative project on Blockchains to track the food items right from the farms to plates. According to WHO, 600 million people across the globe suffer illness due to contaminated food and around 420,100 of them die due to the related diseases (IBM, 2016). The food suppliers and government incur heavy losses as the food gets contaminated during the transit process. Globally, there was a lack of proper technology to trace the quality of highly perishable food items while it is being transported. IBM came up with a blockchain-based approach to make the food chain transparent, traceable and trustworthy. Blockchains will provide a timely digital tracking of food items while it is being transported and the suppliers or logistics providers cannot alter the immutable public ledger of blockchains (Kralingen, 2016). The digital product information of food such as farm origination details, batch numbers, factory and processing data, expiration dates, storage temperatures and shipping detail are digitally connected and the information is entered into the immutable blockchain along every step of the process (IBM, 2016). This will also help the retailers to properly manage the shelf-life of the food items and reduces the risk of contamination. In future, the blockchain-based food supply chain will drastically reduce the wastage of food due to contamination and transportation delays. Moreover, this can help the governments is providing better healthcare facilities as healthy food can nurture healthy citizens.

REFERENCES

Augur. (2016). *Augur: Reference Client*. Retrieved from http://docs.augur.net/#overview

Bogdan, D. (2016). *Decentralised social media: doing it the blockchain way*. Retrieved from http://www.coinfox.info/news/reviews/5846-blockchain-social-media

Crosby, M., Nachippan, Pattanayak P., Verma S., & Kalyanaraman, V. (2015). *BlockChain Technology Beyond Bitcoin*. Sutardja Center for Entrepreneurship & Technology Technical Report.

IBM. (2016). *Walmart, IBM and Tsinghua University Explore the Use of Blockchain to Help Bring Safer Food to Dinner Tables Across China*. Retrieved from https://www-03.ibm.com/press/us/en/pressrelease/50816.wss

IBM Blockchain. (2016). *The Hyperledger Project*. Retrieved from http://www.ibm.com/blockchain/hyperledger.html

Kate. (2016). *Blockchain Will Define the Future of Social Networks*. Retrieved from https://letstalkpayments.com/blockchain-will-define-the-future-of-social-networks/

Kralingen, B. (2016). *How Blockchain Could Help To Make The Food We Eat Safer... Around The World.* IBM. Retrieved from http://www.forbes.com/sites/ibm/2016/11/01/how-blockchain-could-help-to-make-the-food-we-eat-safer-around-the-world/#41fbbe3d67df

Lazooz. (2016). *Lazooz: White Paper.* Retrieved from http://lazooz.org/whitepaper.html

O'Dair, M., Beaven, Z., Neilson, D., Osborne, R., & Pacifico, P. (2016). *Music on the blockchain.* Academic Press.

Panikkar, S., Nair, S., Brody, P., & Pureswaran, V. (2014). *ADEPT: An IoT Practitioner Perspective.* IBM Institute for Business Value.

Pilkington, M. (2016). *Blockchain technology: principles and applications. In Research Handbook on Digital Transformations.* Edward Elgar.

Prisco, G. (2016a). *MIT Media Lab Releases Code for Digital Certificates on the Blockchain.* Retrieved from https://bitcoinmagazine.com/articles/mit-media-lab-releases-code-for-digital-certificates-on-the-blockchain-1465404945

Prisco, G. (2016b). *Slock.it to Introduce Smart Locks Linked to Smart Ethereum Contracts, Decentralize the Sharing Economy.* Retrieved from https://bitcoinmagazine.com/articles/slock-it-to-introduce-smart-locks-linked-to-smart-ethereum-contracts-decentralize-the-sharing-economy-1446746719

Redman, J. (2015). *Neureal: Bringing Artificial Intelligence to the People.* Retrieved from https://cointelegraph.com/news/neureal-bringing-artificial-intelligence-to-the-people

Shieber, J. (2015). *Microsoft Partners With ConsenSys To Use Ethereum To Provide Blockchain-As-A-Service.* Retrieved from https://techcrunch.com/2015/10/28/microsoft-partners-with-consensys-to-use-ethereum-to-provide-blockchain-as-a-service/

Stratumn. (2016). *Stratumn and Deloitte unveil blockchain-based micro-insurance PoC.* Retrieved from https://www.finextra.com/pressarticle/65264/stratumn-and-deloitte-unveil-blockchain-based-micro-insurance-poc

Swan, M. (2015). Blockchain thinking: The brain as a dac (decentralized autonomous organization).*Texas Bitcoin Conference.*

Tapscott, D., & Tapscott, A. (2016). *How Blockchain Technology Can Reinvent The Power Grid.* Retrieved from http://fortune.com/2016/05/15/blockchain-reinvents-power-grid/

Tieron. (2016). *Blockchain Healthcare 2016 Report – Promise & Pitfalls.* Retrieved from https://tierion.com/blog/blockchain-healthcare-2016-report/

Walport, M. (2016). Distributed Ledger Technology: Beyond Blockchain. UK Government Office for Science, Tech. Rep, 19.

Wilkinson, S., Lowry, J., & Boshevski, T. (2014). *Metadisk a blockchain-based decentralized file storage application.* Technical Report. Retrieved from http://metadisk. org/metadisk.pdf

Conclusion

From the time of inception, Blockchain technology has gained considerable attention among researchers and technocrats due to its mind-blowing application potential in a variety of real world scenarios. Presently, most of them consider blockchain as an important technical invention after 'The Internet' which could disrupt most of the existing technologies and business domains. The compelling features of blockchains, such as immutability, trust-free nature, resilience to illegal modifications, cryptographic hashing, consensus based decision making, publicly verifiable ledger capability etc., makes this technology one of the most promising technical breakthrough capable of addressing many avenues of computational requirement in real world problem solving. Moreover, the decentralized computing paradigm got re-invented with the advent of blockchains due to its merits as mentioned above over the conventional decentralization mechanisms.

The blockchain revolution is now reaching new heights with the release of Smart contracts and programmable blockchains such as Ethereum. These technologies further enhance the blockchains to mature it as a dependable platform for developing decentralized application which could be a boon to every business domain. The future of computing world would be definitely disrupted by the blockchain technology with its exponential potential supporting the growth of smart, resilient, trust-free decentralized applications. In this book, we have made an effort to describe the basics of blockchains and its current and forthcoming applications. We are sure that most of the concepts which are in a nascent state at the time of writing this book will graduate to potentially disruptive applications solving many real world problems in near future.

Appendix 1: Ethereum Clients

1. **Go-Ethereum:** The go-ethereum client is commonly referred to as geth, which is the the command line interface for running a full ethereum node implemented in Go.
2. **Pyethapp:** Pyethapp is the python-based client implementing the Ethereum cryptoeconomic state machine. The python implementation aims to provide an easily hackable and extendable codebase
3. **Ethereum(J):** Ethereum(J) is a pure-Java implementation of the Ethereum protocol. It is provided as a library that can be embedded in any Java/Scala project and to provide full support for Ethereum protocol and sub-services.
4. **EthereumH:** This package provides a tool written in Haskell to allow you to connect to the Ethereum blockchain
5. **Parity:** Parity claims to be the world's fastest and lightest Ethereum client. It is written in the Rust language, which offers improved reliability, performance, and code clarity. Parity is being developed by Ethcore, which was founded by several members of the Ethereum Foundation.
6. **Ruby-Ethereum:** Ruby-ethereum is an implementation of the Ethereum Virtual Machine written in Ruby.

Appendix 2: Libraries for Ethereum Clients

1. **Web3.js:** This is the Ethereum compatible JavaScript API which implements the Generic JSON RPC spec. It's available on npm as a node module, for bower and component as an embeddable js and as a meteor. js package

2. **Web3j:** web3j is a lightweight Java library for integrating with clients (nodes) on the Ethereum network that supports all JSON-RPC method types

3. **Nethereum:** Nethereum is the .Net integration library for Ethereum, it allows you to interact with Ethereum clients like goethereum, cpp-ethereum or Parity using RPC

4. **Ethereum-Ruby:** Ethereum-ruby is a pure-Ruby JSON-RPC wrapper for communicating with an Ethereum node. To use this library you will need to have a running Ethereum node with IPC support enabled (default).

Related Readings

To continue IGI Global's long-standing tradition of advancing innovation through emerging research, please find below a compiled list of recommended IGI Global book chapters and journal articles in the areas of data storage, decentralized computing, and the internet of things. These related readings will provide additional information and guidance to further enrich your knowledge and assist you with your own research.

Abidi, N., Bandyopadhayay, A., & Gupta, V. (2017). Sustainable Supply Chain Management: A Three Dimensional Framework and Performance Metric for Indian IT Product Companies. *International Journal of Information Systems and Supply Chain Management, 10*(1), 29–52. doi:10.4018/IJISSCM.2017010103

Achahbar, O., & Abid, M. R. (2015). The Impact of Virtualization on High Performance Computing Clustering in the Cloud. *International Journal of Distributed Systems and Technologies, 6*(4), 65–81. doi:10.4018/IJDST.2015100104

Adhikari, M., Das, A., & Mukherjee, A. (2016). Utility Computing and Its Utilization. In G. Deka, G. Siddesh, K. Srinivasa, & L. Patnaik (Eds.), *Emerging Research Surrounding Power Consumption and Performance Issues in Utility Computing* (pp. 1–21). Hershey, PA: IGI Global. doi:10.4018/978-1-4666-8853-7.ch001

Aggarwal, S., & Nayak, A. (2016). Mobile Big Data: A New Frontier of Innovation. In J. Aguado, C. Feijóo, & I. Martínez (Eds.), *Emerging Perspectives on the Mobile Content Evolution* (pp. 138–158). Hershey, PA: IGI Global. doi:10.4018/978-1-4666-8838-4.ch008

Akherfi, K., Harroud, H., & Gerndt, M. (2016). A Mobile Cloud Middleware to Support Mobility and Cloud Interoperability. *International Journal of Adaptive, Resilient and Autonomic Systems, 7*(1), 41–58. doi:10.4018/IJARAS.2016010103

Al-Hamami, M. A. (2015). The Impact of Big Data on Security. In A. Al-Hamami & G. Waleed al-Saadoon (Eds.), *Handbook of Research on Threat Detection and Countermeasures in Network Security* (pp. 276–298). Hershey, PA: IGI Global. doi:10.4018/978-1-4666-6583-5.ch015

Al Jabri, H. A., Al-Badi, A. H., & Ali, O. (2017). Exploring the Usage of Big Data Analytical Tools in Telecommunication Industry in Oman. *Information Resources Management Journal, 30*(1), 1–14. doi:10.4018/IRMJ.2017010101

Alohali, B. (2016). Security in Cloud of Things (CoT). In Z. Ma (Ed.), *Managing Big Data in Cloud Computing Environments* (pp. 46–70). Hershey, PA: IGI Global. doi:10.4018/978-1-4666-9834-5.ch003

Alohali, B. (2017). Detection Protocol of Possible Crime Scenes Using Internet of Things (IoT). In M. Moore (Ed.), *Cybersecurity Breaches and Issues Surrounding Online Threat Protection* (pp. 175–196). Hershey, PA: IGI Global. doi:10.4018/978-1-5225-1941-6.ch008

AlZain, M. A., Li, A. S., Soh, B., & Pardede, E. (2015). Multi-Cloud Data Management using Shamirs Secret Sharing and Quantum Byzantine Agreement Schemes. *International Journal of Cloud Applications and Computing, 5*(3), 35–52. doi:10.4018/IJCAC.2015070103

Armstrong, S., & Yampolskiy, R. V. (2017). Security Solutions for Intelligent and Complex Systems. In M. Dawson, M. Eltayeb, & M. Omar (Eds.), *Security Solutions for Hyperconnectivity and the Internet of Things* (pp. 37–88). Hershey, PA: IGI Global. doi:10.4018/978-1-5225-0741-3.ch003

Attasena, V., Harbi, N., & Darmont, J. (2015). A Novel Multi-Secret Sharing Approach for Secure Data Warehousing and On-Line Analysis Processing in the Cloud. *International Journal of Data Warehousing and Mining, 11*(2), 22–43. doi:10.4018/ijdwm.2015040102

Awad, W. S., & Abdullah, H. M. (2014). Improving the Security of Storage Systems: Bahrain Case Study. *International Journal of Mobile Computing and Multimedia Communications, 6*(3), 75–105. doi:10.4018/IJMCMC.2014070104

Bagui, S., & Nguyen, L. T. (2015). Database Sharding: To Provide Fault Tolerance and Scalability of Big Data on the Cloud. *International Journal of Cloud Applications and Computing*, *5*(2), 36–52. doi:10.4018/IJCAC.2015040103

Barbierato, E., Gribaudo, M., & Iacono, M. (2016). Modeling and Evaluating the Effects of Big Data Storage Resource Allocation in Global Scale Cloud Architectures. *International Journal of Data Warehousing and Mining*, *12*(2), 1–20. doi:10.4018/IJDWM.2016040101

Barbosa, J. L., Barbosa, D. N., Rigo, S. J., Machado de Oliveira, J., & Junior, S. A. (2017). Collaborative Learning on Decentralized Ubiquitous Environments. In L. Tomei (Ed.), *Exploring the New Era of Technology-Infused Education* (pp. 141–157). Hershey, PA: IGI Global. doi:10.4018/978-1-5225-1709-2.ch009

Benmounah, Z., Meshoul, S., & Batouche, M. (2017). Scalable Differential Evolutionary Clustering Algorithm for Big Data Using Map-Reduce Paradigm. *International Journal of Applied Metaheuristic Computing*, *8*(1), 45–60. doi:10.4018/IJAMC.2017010103

Bhadoria, R. S. (2016). Performance of Enterprise Architecture in Utility Computing. In G. Deka, G. Siddesh, K. Srinivasa, & L. Patnaik (Eds.), *Emerging Research Surrounding Power Consumption and Performance Issues in Utility Computing* (pp. 44–68). Hershey, PA: IGI Global. doi:10.4018/978-1-4666-8853-7.ch003

Bhardwaj, A. (2017). Solutions for Securing End User Data over the Cloud Deployed Applications. In M. Moore (Ed.), *Cybersecurity Breaches and Issues Surrounding Online Threat Protection* (pp. 198–218). Hershey, PA: IGI Global. doi:10.4018/978-1-5225-1941-6.ch009

Bibi, S., Katsaros, D., & Bozanis, P. (2015). Cloud Computing Economics. In V. Díaz, J. Lovelle, & B. García-Bustelo (Eds.), *Handbook of Research on Innovations in Systems and Software Engineering* (pp. 125–149). Hershey, PA: IGI Global. doi:10.4018/978-1-4666-6359-6.ch005

Bihl, T. J., Young, W. A. II, & Weckman, G. R. (2016). Defining, Understanding, and Addressing Big Data. *International Journal of Business Analytics*, *3*(2), 1–32. doi:10.4018/IJBAN.2016040101

Related Readings

Bimonte, S., Sautot, L., Journaux, L., & Faivre, B. (2017). Multidimensional Model Design using Data Mining: A Rapid Prototyping Methodology. *International Journal of Data Warehousing and Mining, 13*(1), 1–35. doi:10.4018/IJDWM.2017010101

Bruno, G. (2017). A Dataflow-Oriented Modeling Approach to Business Processes. *International Journal of Human Capital and Information Technology Professionals, 8*(1), 51–65. doi:10.4018/IJHCITP.2017010104

Chande, S. V. (2014). Cloud Database Systems: NoSQL, NewSQL, and Hybrid. In P. Raj & G. Deka (Eds.), *Handbook of Research on Cloud Infrastructures for Big Data Analytics* (pp. 216–231). Hershey, PA: IGI Global. doi:10.4018/978-1-4666-5864-6.ch009

Cordeschi, N., Shojafar, M., Amendola, D., & Baccarelli, E. (2015). Energy-Saving QoS Resource Management of Virtualized Networked Data Centers for Big Data Stream Computing. In S. Bagchi (Ed.), *Emerging Research in Cloud Distributed Computing Systems* (pp. 122–155). Hershey, PA: IGI Global. doi:10.4018/978-1-4666-8213-9.ch004

Costan, A. A., Iancu, B., Rasa, P. C., Radu, A., Peculea, A., & Dadarlat, V. T. (2017). Intercloud: Delivering Innovative Cloud Services. In I. Hosu & I. Iancu (Eds.), *Digital Entrepreneurship and Global Innovation* (pp. 59–78). Hershey, PA: IGI Global. doi:10.4018/978-1-5225-0953-0.ch004

Croatti, A., Ricci, A., & Viroli, M. (2017). Towards a Mobile Augmented Reality System for Emergency Management: The Case of SAFE. *International Journal of Distributed Systems and Technologies, 8*(1), 46–58. doi:10.4018/IJDST.2017010104

David-West, O. (2016). Information and Communications Technology (ICT) and the Supply Chain. In B. Christiansen (Ed.), *Handbook of Research on Global Supply Chain Management* (pp. 495–515). Hershey, PA: IGI Global. doi:10.4018/978-1-4666-9639-6.ch028

Dawson, M. (2017). Exploring Secure Computing for the Internet of Things, Internet of Everything, Web of Things, and Hyperconnectivity. In M. Dawson, M. Eltayeb, & M. Omar (Eds.), *Security Solutions for Hyperconnectivity and the Internet of Things* (pp. 1–12). Hershey, PA: IGI Global. doi:10.4018/978-1-5225-0741-3.ch001

Delgado, J. C. (2015). An Interoperability Framework for Enterprise Applications in Cloud Environments. In N. Rao (Ed.), *Enterprise Management Strategies in the Era of Cloud Computing* (pp. 26–59). Hershey, PA: IGI Global. doi:10.4018/978-1-4666-8339-6.ch002

Dhal, S. K., Verma, H., & Addya, S. K. (2017). Resource and Energy Efficient Virtual Machine Migration in Cloud Data Centers. In A. Turuk, B. Sahoo, & S. Addya (Eds.), *Resource Management and Efficiency in Cloud Computing Environments* (pp. 210–238). Hershey, PA: IGI Global. doi:10.4018/978-1-5225-1721-4.ch009

Duggirala, S. (2014). Big Data Architecture: Storage and Computation. In P. Raj & G. Deka (Eds.), *Handbook of Research on Cloud Infrastructures for Big Data Analytics* (pp. 129–156). Hershey, PA: IGI Global. doi:10.4018/978-1-4666-5864-6.ch006

Easton, J., & Parmar, R. (2017). Navigating Your Way to the Hybrid Cloud. In J. Chen, Y. Zhang, & R. Gottschalk (Eds.), *Handbook of Research on End-to-End Cloud Computing Architecture Design* (pp. 15–38). Hershey, PA: IGI Global. doi:10.4018/978-1-5225-0759-8.ch002

Elkabbany, G. F., & Rasslan, M. (2017). Security Issues in Distributed Computing System Models. In M. Dawson, M. Eltayeb, & M. Omar (Eds.), *Security Solutions for Hyperconnectivity and the Internet of Things* (pp. 211–259). Hershey, PA: IGI Global. doi:10.4018/978-1-5225-0741-3.ch009

Elkhodr, M., Shahrestani, S., & Cheung, H. (2016). Wireless Enabling Technologies for the Internet of Things. In Q. Hassan (Ed.), *Innovative Research and Applications in Next-Generation High Performance Computing* (pp. 368–396). Hershey, PA: IGI Global. doi:10.4018/978-1-5225-0287-6.ch015

Elkhodr, M., Shahrestani, S., & Cheung, H. (2017). Internet of Things Research Challenges. In M. Dawson, M. Eltayeb, & M. Omar (Eds.), *Security Solutions for Hyperconnectivity and the Internet of Things* (pp. 13–36). Hershey, PA: IGI Global. doi:10.4018/978-1-5225-0741-3.ch002

Erturk, E. (2017). Cloud Computing and Cybersecurity Issues Facing Local Enterprises. In M. Moore (Ed.), *Cybersecurity Breaches and Issues Surrounding Online Threat Protection* (pp. 219–247). Hershey, PA: IGI Global. doi:10.4018/978-1-5225-1941-6.ch010

Ferreira da Silva, R., Glatard, T., & Desprez, F. (2015). Self-Management of Operational Issues for Grid Computing: The Case of the Virtual Imaging Platform. In S. Bagchi (Ed.), *Emerging Research in Cloud Distributed Computing Systems* (pp. 187–221). Hershey, PA: IGI Global. doi:10.4018/978-1-4666-8213-9.ch006

Fu, S., He, L., Liao, X., Huang, C., Li, K., & Chang, C. (2015). Analyzing and Boosting the Data Availability in Decentralized Online Social Networks. *International Journal of Web Services Research*, *12*(2), 47–72. doi:10.4018/IJWSR.2015040103

Gao, F., & Zhao, Q. (2014). Big Data Based Logistics Data Mining Platform: Architecture and Implementation. *International Journal of Interdisciplinary Telecommunications and Networking*, *6*(4), 24–34. doi:10.4018/IJITN.2014100103

Gudivada, V. N., Nandigam, J., & Paris, J. (2015). Programming Paradigms in High Performance Computing. In R. Segall, J. Cook, & Q. Zhang (Eds.), *Research and Applications in Global Supercomputing* (pp. 303–330). Hershey, PA: IGI Global. doi:10.4018/978-1-4666-7461-5.ch013

Hagos, D. H. (2016). Software-Defined Networking for Scalable Cloud-based Services to Improve System Performance of Hadoop-based Big Data Applications. *International Journal of Grid and High Performance Computing*, *8*(2), 1–22. doi:10.4018/IJGHPC.2016040101

Hallappanavar, V. L., & Birje, M. N. (2017). Trust Management in Cloud Computing. In M. Dawson, M. Eltayeb, & M. Omar (Eds.), *Security Solutions for Hyperconnectivity and the Internet of Things* (pp. 151–183). Hershey, PA: IGI Global. doi:10.4018/978-1-5225-0741-3.ch007

Hameur Laine, A., & Brahimi, S. (2017). Background on Context-Aware Computing Systems. In C. Reis & M. Maximiano (Eds.), *Internet of Things and Advanced Application in Healthcare* (pp. 1–31). Hershey, PA: IGI Global. doi:10.4018/978-1-5225-1820-4.ch001

Hamidi, H. (2017). A Model for Impact of Organizational Project Benefits Management and its Impact on End User. *Journal of Organizational and End User Computing*, *29*(1), 51–65. doi:10.4018/JOEUC.2017010104

Hamidine, H., & Mahmood, A. (2017). Cloud Computing Data Storage Security Based on Different Encryption Schemes. In J. Chen, Y. Zhang, & R. Gottschalk (Eds.), *Handbook of Research on End-to-End Cloud Computing Architecture Design* (pp. 189–221). Hershey, PA: IGI Global. doi:10.4018/978-1-5225-0759-8.ch009

Hamidine, H., & Mahmood, A. (2017). Cloud Computing Data Storage Security Based on Different Encryption Schemes. In J. Chen, Y. Zhang, & R. Gottschalk (Eds.), *Handbook of Research on End-to-End Cloud Computing Architecture Design* (pp. 189–221). Hershey, PA: IGI Global. doi:10.4018/978-1-5225-0759-8.ch009

Hao, Y., & Helo, P. (2015). Cloud Manufacturing towards Sustainable Management. In F. Soliman (Ed.), *Business Transformation and Sustainability through Cloud System Implementation* (pp. 121–139). Hershey, PA: IGI Global. doi:10.4018/978-1-4666-6445-6.ch009

Hasan, N., & Rahman, A. A. (2017). Ranking the Factors that Impact Customers Online Participation in Value Co-creation in Service Sector Using Analytic Hierarchy Process. *International Journal of Information Systems in the Service Sector*, 9(1), 37–53. doi:10.4018/IJISSS.2017010103

Hashemi, S., Monfaredi, K., & Hashemi, S. Y. (2015). Cloud Computing for Secure Services in E-Government Architecture. *Journal of Information Technology Research*, 8(1), 43–61. doi:10.4018/JITR.2015010104

Hayajneh, S. M. (2015). Cloud Computing SaaS Paradigm for Efficient Modelling of Solar Features and Activities. *International Journal of Cloud Applications and Computing*, 5(3), 20–34. doi:10.4018/IJCAC.2015070102

Huang, L. K. (2017). A Cultural Model of Online Banking Adoption: Long-Term Orientation Perspective. *Journal of Organizational and End User Computing*, 29(1), 1–22. doi:10.4018/JOEUC.2017010101

Jacob, G., & Annamalai, M. (2017). Secure Storage and Transmission of Healthcare Records. In V. Tiwari, B. Tiwari, R. Thakur, & S. Gupta (Eds.), *Pattern and Data Analysis in Healthcare Settings* (pp. 7–34). Hershey, PA: IGI Global. doi:10.4018/978-1-5225-0536-5.ch002

Jadon, K. S., Mudgal, P., & Bhadoria, R. S. (2016). Optimization and Management of Resource in Utility Computing. In G. Deka, G. Siddesh, K. Srinivasa, & L. Patnaik (Eds.), *Emerging Research Surrounding Power Consumption and Performance Issues in Utility Computing* (pp. 22–43). Hershey, PA: IGI Global. doi:10.4018/978-1-4666-8853-7.ch002

Jararweh, Y., Al-Sharqawi, O., Abdulla, N., Tawalbeh, L., & Alhammouri, M. (2014). High-Throughput Encryption for Cloud Computing Storage System. *International Journal of Cloud Applications and Computing*, 4(2), 1–14. doi:10.4018/ijcac.2014040101

Jha, M., Jha, S., & O'Brien, L. (2017). Social Media and Big Data: A Conceptual Foundation for Organizations. In R. Chugh (Ed.), *Harnessing Social Media as a Knowledge Management Tool* (pp. 315–332). Hershey, PA: IGI Global. doi:10.4018/978-1-5225-0495-5.ch015

Kantarci, B., & Mouftah, H. T. (2015). Sensing as a Service in Cloud-Centric Internet of Things Architecture. In T. Soyata (Ed.), *Enabling Real-Time Mobile Cloud Computing through Emerging Technologies* (pp. 83–115). Hershey, PA: IGI Global. doi:10.4018/978-1-4666-8662-5.ch003

Kasemsap, K. (2015). The Role of Cloud Computing Adoption in Global Business. In V. Chang, R. Walters, & G. Wills (Eds.), *Delivery and Adoption of Cloud Computing Services in Contemporary Organizations* (pp. 26–55). Hershey, PA: IGI Global. doi:10.4018/978-1-4666-8210-8.ch002

Kasemsap, K. (2015). The Role of Cloud Computing in Global Supply Chain. In N. Rao (Ed.), *Enterprise Management Strategies in the Era of Cloud Computing* (pp. 192–219). Hershey, PA: IGI Global. doi:10.4018/978-1-4666-8339-6.ch009

Kasemsap, K. (2017). Mastering Intelligent Decision Support Systems in Enterprise Information Management. In G. Sreedhar (Ed.), *Web Data Mining and the Development of Knowledge-Based Decision Support Systems* (pp. 35–56). Hershey, PA: IGI Global. doi:10.4018/978-1-5225-1877-8.ch004

Kaukalias, T., & Chatzimisios, P. (2015). Internet of Things (IoT). In M. Khosrow-Pour (Ed.), *Encyclopedia of Information Science and Technology* (3rd ed.; pp. 7623–7632). Hershey, PA: IGI Global. doi:10.4018/978-1-4666-5888-2.ch751

Kavoura, A., & Koziol, L. (2017). Polish Firms' Innovation Capability for Competitiveness via Information Technologies and Social Media Implementation. In A. Vlachvei, O. Notta, K. Karantininis, & N. Tsounis (Eds.), *Factors Affecting Firm Competitiveness and Performance in the Modern Business World* (pp. 191–222). Hershey, PA: IGI Global. doi:10.4018/978-1-5225-0843-4.ch007

Khan, I. U., Hameed, Z., & Khan, S. U. (2017). Understanding Online Banking Adoption in a Developing Country: UTAUT2 with Cultural Moderators. *Journal of Global Information Management*, *25*(1), 43–65. doi:10.4018/JGIM.2017010103

Kirci, P. (2017). Ubiquitous and Cloud Computing: Ubiquitous Computing. In A. Turuk, B. Sahoo, & S. Addya (Eds.), *Resource Management and Efficiency in Cloud Computing Environments* (pp. 1–32). Hershey, PA: IGI Global. doi:10.4018/978-1-5225-1721-4.ch001

Kofahi, I., & Alryalat, H. (2017). Enterprise Resource Planning (ERP) Implementation Approaches and the Performance of Procure-to-Pay Business Processes: (Field Study in Companies that Implement Oracle ERP in Jordan). *International Journal of Information Technology Project Management*, *8*(1), 55–71. doi:10.4018/IJITPM.2017010104

Koumaras, H., Damaskos, C., Diakoumakos, G., Kourtis, M., Xilouris, G., Gardikis, G., & Siakoulis, T. et al. (2015). Virtualization Evolution: From IT Infrastructure Abstraction of Cloud Computing to Virtualization of Network Functions. In G. Mastorakis, C. Mavromoustakis, & E. Pallis (Eds.), *Resource Management of Mobile Cloud Computing Networks and Environments* (pp. 279–306). Hershey, PA: IGI Global. doi:10.4018/978-1-4666-8225-2.ch010

Kuada, E. (2017). Security and Trust in Cloud Computing. In M. Dawson, M. Eltayeb, & M. Omar (Eds.), *Security Solutions for Hyperconnectivity and the Internet of Things* (pp. 184–210). Hershey, PA: IGI Global. doi:10.4018/978-1-5225-0741-3.ch008

Kumar, D., Sahoo, B., & Mandal, T. (2015). Heuristic Task Consolidation Techniques for Energy Efficient Cloud Computing. In N. Rao (Ed.), *Enterprise Management Strategies in the Era of Cloud Computing* (pp. 238–260). Hershey, PA: IGI Global. doi:10.4018/978-1-4666-8339-6.ch011

Related Readings

Lee, C. K., Cao, Y., & Ng, K. H. (2017). Big Data Analytics for Predictive Maintenance Strategies. In H. Chan, N. Subramanian, & M. Abdulrahman (Eds.), *Supply Chain Management in the Big Data Era* (pp. 50–74). Hershey, PA: IGI Global. doi:10.4018/978-1-5225-0956-1.ch004

Liao, W. (2016). Application of Hadoop in the Document Storage Management System for Telecommunication Enterprise. *International Journal of Interdisciplinary Telecommunications and Networking*, 8(2), 58–68. doi:10.4018/IJITN.2016040106

Liew, C. S., Ang, J. M., Goh, Y. T., Koh, W. K., Tan, S. Y., & Teh, R. Y. (2017). Factors Influencing Consumer Acceptance of Internet of Things Technology. In N. Suki (Ed.), *Handbook of Research on Leveraging Consumer Psychology for Effective Customer Engagement* (pp. 186–201). Hershey, PA: IGI Global. doi:10.4018/978-1-5225-0746-8.ch012

Lytras, M. D., Raghavan, V., & Damiani, E. (2017). Big Data and Data Analytics Research: From Metaphors to Value Space for Collective Wisdom in Human Decision Making and Smart Machines. *International Journal on Semantic Web and Information Systems*, 13(1), 1–10. doi:10.4018/IJSWIS.2017010101

Mabe, L. K., & Oladele, O. I. (2017). Application of Information Communication Technologies for Agricultural Development through Extension Services: A Review. In T. Tossy (Ed.), *Information Technology Integration for Socio-Economic Development* (pp. 52–101). Hershey, PA: IGI Global. doi:10.4018/978-1-5225-0539-6.ch003

Machaka, P., & Nelwamondo, F. (2016). Data Mining Techniques for Distributed Denial of Service Attacks Detection in the Internet of Things: A Research Survey. In O. Isafiade & A. Bagula (Eds.), *Data Mining Trends and Applications in Criminal Science and Investigations* (pp. 275–334). Hershey, PA: IGI Global. doi:10.4018/978-1-5225-0463-4.ch010

Manohari, P. K., & Ray, N. K. (2017). A Comprehensive Study of Security in Cloud Computing. In N. Ray & A. Turuk (Eds.), *Handbook of Research on Advanced Wireless Sensor Network Applications, Protocols, and Architectures* (pp. 386–412). Hershey, PA: IGI Global. doi:10.4018/978-1-5225-0486-3.ch016

Manvi, S. S., & Hegde, N. (2017). Vehicular Cloud Computing Challenges and Security. In S. Bhattacharyya, N. Das, D. Bhattacharjee, & A. Mukherjee (Eds.), *Handbook of Research on Recent Developments in Intelligent Communication Application* (pp. 344–365). Hershey, PA: IGI Global. doi:10.4018/978-1-5225-1785-6.ch013

McKelvey, N., Curran, K., & Subaginy, N. (2015). The Internet of Things. In M. Khosrow-Pour (Ed.), *Encyclopedia of Information Science and Technology* (3rd ed.; pp. 5777–5783). Hershey, PA: IGI Global. doi:10.4018/978-1-4666-5888-2.ch570

Meddah, I. H., Belkadi, K., & Boudia, M. A. (2017). Efficient Implementation of Hadoop MapReduce based Business Process Dataflow. *International Journal of Decision Support System Technology*, *9*(1), 49–60. doi:10.4018/IJDSST.2017010104

Meghanathan, N. (2015). Virtualization as the Catalyst for Cloud Computing. In M. Khosrow-Pour (Ed.), *Encyclopedia of Information Science and Technology* (3rd ed.; pp. 1096–1110). Hershey, PA: IGI Global. doi:10.4018/978-1-4666-5888-2.ch105

Mehenni, T. (2017). Geographic Knowledge Discovery in Multiple Spatial Databases. In S. Faiz & K. Mahmoudi (Eds.), *Handbook of Research on Geographic Information Systems Applications and Advancements* (pp. 344–366). Hershey, PA: IGI Global. doi:10.4018/978-1-5225-0937-0.ch013

Mehrotra, S., & Kohli, S. (2017). Data Clustering and Various Clustering Approaches. In S. Bhattacharyya, S. De, I. Pan, & P. Dutta (Eds.), *Intelligent Multidimensional Data Clustering and Analysis* (pp. 90–108). Hershey, PA: IGI Global. doi:10.4018/978-1-5225-1776-4.ch004

Meralto, C., Moura, J., & Marinheiro, R. (2017). Wireless Mesh Sensor Networks with Mobile Devices: A Comprehensive Review. In N. Ray & A. Turuk (Eds.), *Handbook of Research on Advanced Wireless Sensor Network Applications, Protocols, and Architectures* (pp. 129–155). Hershey, PA: IGI Global. doi:10.4018/978-1-5225-0486-3.ch005

Moradbeikie, A., Abrishami, S., & Abbasi, H. (2016). Creating Time-Limited Attributes for Time-Limited Services in Cloud Computing. *International Journal of Information Security and Privacy*, *10*(4), 44–57. doi:10.4018/IJISP.2016100103

Mourtzoukos, K., Kefalakis, N., & Soldatos, J. (2015). Open Source Object Directory Services for Inter-Enterprise Tracking and Tracing Applications. In I. Lee (Ed.), *RFID Technology Integration for Business Performance Improvement* (pp. 80–97). Hershey, PA: IGI Global. doi:10.4018/978-1-4666-6308-4.ch004

Mugisha, E., Zhang, G., El Abidine, M. Z., & Eugene, M. (2017). A TPM-based Secure Multi-Cloud Storage Architecture grounded on Erasure Codes. *International Journal of Information Security and Privacy, 11*(1), 52–64. doi:10.4018/IJISP.2017010104

Munir, K. (2017). Security Model for Mobile Cloud Database as a Service (DBaaS). In K. Munir (Ed.), *Security Management in Mobile Cloud Computing* (pp. 169–180). Hershey, PA: IGI Global. doi:10.4018/978-1-5225-0602-7.ch008

Murugaiyan, S. R., Chandramohan, D., Vengattaraman, T., & Dhavachelvan, P. (2014). A Generic Privacy Breach Preventing Methodology for Cloud Based Web Service. *International Journal of Grid and High Performance Computing, 6*(3), 53–84. doi:10.4018/ijghpc.2014070104

Naeem, M. A., & Jamil, N. (2015). Online Processing of End-User Data in Real-Time Data Warehousing. In M. Usman (Ed.), *Improving Knowledge Discovery through the Integration of Data Mining Techniques* (pp. 13–31). Hershey, PA: IGI Global. doi:10.4018/978-1-4666-8513-0.ch002

Nayak, P. (2017). Internet of Things Services, Applications, Issues, and Challenges. In N. Ray & A. Turuk (Eds.), *Handbook of Research on Advanced Wireless Sensor Network Applications, Protocols, and Architectures* (pp. 353–368). Hershey, PA: IGI Global. doi:10.4018/978-1-5225-0486-3.ch014

Nekaj, E. L. (2017). The Crowd Economy: From the Crowd to Businesses to Public Administrations and Multinational Companies. In W. Vassallo (Ed.), *Crowdfunding for Sustainable Entrepreneurship and Innovation* (pp. 1–19). Hershey, PA: IGI Global. doi:10.4018/978-1-5225-0568-6.ch001

Omar, M. (2015). Cloud Computing Security: Abuse and Nefarious Use of Cloud Computing. In K. Munir, M. Al-Mutairi, & L. Mohammed (Eds.), *Handbook of Research on Security Considerations in Cloud Computing* (pp. 30–38). Hershey, PA: IGI Global. doi:10.4018/978-1-4666-8387-7.ch002

Orike, S., & Brown, D. (2016). Big Data Management: An Investigation into Wireless and Cloud Computing. *International Journal of Interdisciplinary Telecommunications and Networking*, 8(4), 34–50. doi:10.4018/IJITN.2016100104

Ouf, S., & Nasr, M. (2015). Cloud Computing: The Future of Big Data Management. *International Journal of Cloud Applications and Computing*, 5(2), 53–61. doi:10.4018/IJCAC.2015040104

Ozpinar, A., & Yarkan, S. (2016). Vehicle to Cloud: Big Data for Environmental Sustainability, Energy, and Traffic Management. In M. Singh, & D. G. (Eds.), Effective Big Data Management and Opportunities for Implementation (pp. 182-201). Hershey, PA: IGI Global. doi:10.4018/978-1-5225-0182-4.ch012

Pal, A., & Kumar, M. (2017). Collaborative Filtering Based Data Mining for Large Data. In V. Bhatnagar (Ed.), *Collaborative Filtering Using Data Mining and Analysis* (pp. 115–127). Hershey, PA: IGI Global. doi:10.4018/978-1-5225-0489-4.ch006

Pal, K., & Karakostas, B. (2016). A Game-Based Approach for Simulation and Design of Supply Chains. In T. Kramberger, V. Potočan, & V. Ipavec (Eds.), *Sustainable Logistics and Strategic Transportation Planning* (pp. 1–23). Hershey, PA: IGI Global. doi:10.4018/978-1-5225-0001-8.ch001

Panda, S. (2017). Security Issues and Challenges in Internet of Things. In N. Ray & A. Turuk (Eds.), *Handbook of Research on Advanced Wireless Sensor Network Applications, Protocols, and Architectures* (pp. 369–385). Hershey, PA: IGI Global. doi:10.4018/978-1-5225-0486-3.ch015

Pandit, S., Milman, I., Oberhofer, M., & Zhou, Y. (2017). Principled Reference Data Management for Big Data and Business Intelligence. *International Journal of Organizational and Collective Intelligence*, 7(1), 47–66. doi:10.4018/IJOCI.2017010104

Paul, A. K., & Sahoo, B. (2017). Dynamic Virtual Machine Placement in Cloud Computing. In A. Turuk, B. Sahoo, & S. Addya (Eds.), *Resource Management and Efficiency in Cloud Computing Environments* (pp. 136–167). Hershey, PA: IGI Global. doi:10.4018/978-1-5225-1721-4.ch006

Petri, I., Diaz-Montes, J., Zou, M., Zamani, A. R., Beach, T. H., Rana, O. F., & Rezgui, Y. et al. (2016). Distributed Multi-Cloud Based Building Data Analytics. In G. Kecskemeti, A. Kertesz, & Z. Nemeth (Eds.), *Developing Interoperable and Federated Cloud Architecture* (pp. 143–169). Hershey, PA: IGI Global. doi:10.4018/978-1-5225-0153-4.ch006

Poleto, T., Heuer de Carvalho, V. D., & Costa, A. P. (2017). The Full Knowledge of Big Data in the Integration of Inter-Organizational Information: An Approach Focused on Decision Making. *International Journal of Decision Support System Technology*, 9(1), 16–31. doi:10.4018/IJDSST.2017010102

Rahman, N., & Iverson, S. (2015). Big Data Business Intelligence in Bank Risk Analysis. *International Journal of Business Intelligence Research*, 6(2), 55–77. doi:10.4018/IJBIR.2015070104

Raj, P. (2014). Big Data Analytics Demystified. In P. Raj & G. Deka (Eds.), *Handbook of Research on Cloud Infrastructures for Big Data Analytics* (pp. 38–73). Hershey, PA: IGI Global. doi:10.4018/978-1-4666-5864-6.ch003

Raj, P. (2014). The Compute Infrastructures for Big Data Analytics. In P. Raj & G. Deka (Eds.), *Handbook of Research on Cloud Infrastructures for Big Data Analytics* (pp. 74–109). Hershey, PA: IGI Global. doi:10.4018/978-1-4666-5864-6.ch004

Raj, P. (2014). The Network Infrastructures for Big Data Analytics. In P. Raj & G. Deka (Eds.), *Handbook of Research on Cloud Infrastructures for Big Data Analytics* (pp. 157–185). Hershey, PA: IGI Global. doi:10.4018/978-1-4666-5864-6.ch007

Raman, A. C. (2014). Storage Infrastructure for Big Data and Cloud. In P. Raj & G. Deka (Eds.), *Handbook of Research on Cloud Infrastructures for Big Data Analytics* (pp. 110–128). Hershey, PA: IGI Global. doi:10.4018/978-1-4666-5864-6.ch005

Rao, A. P. (2017). Discovering Knowledge Hidden in Big Data from Machine-Learning Techniques. In G. Sreedhar (Ed.), *Web Data Mining and the Development of Knowledge-Based Decision Support Systems* (pp. 167–183). Hershey, PA: IGI Global. doi:10.4018/978-1-5225-1877-8.ch010

Rathore, M. M., Paul, A., Ahmad, A., & Jeon, G. (2017). IoT-Based Big Data: From Smart City towards Next Generation Super City Planning. *International Journal on Semantic Web and Information Systems*, *13*(1), 28–47. doi:10.4018/IJSWIS.2017010103

Ratten, V. (2015). An Entrepreneurial Approach to Cloud Computing Design and Application: Technological Innovation and Information System Usage. In S. Aljawarneh (Ed.), *Advanced Research on Cloud Computing Design and Applications* (pp. 1–14). Hershey, PA: IGI Global. doi:10.4018/978-1-4666-8676-2.ch001

Rebekah, R. D., Cheelu, D., & Babu, M. R. (2017). Necessity of Key Aggregation Cryptosystem for Data Sharing in Cloud Computing. In P. Krishna (Ed.), *Emerging Technologies and Applications for Cloud-Based Gaming* (pp. 210–227). Hershey, PA: IGI Global. doi:10.4018/978-1-5225-0546-4.ch010

Rehman, A., Ullah, R., & Abdullah, F. (2015). Big Data Analysis in IoT. In N. Zaman, M. Seliaman, M. Hassan, & F. Marquez (Eds.), *Handbook of Research on Trends and Future Directions in Big Data and Web Intelligence* (pp. 313–327). Hershey, PA: IGI Global. doi:10.4018/978-1-4666-8505-5.ch015

Rehman, M. H., Khan, A. U., & Batool, A. (2016). Big Data Analytics in Mobile and Cloud Computing Environments. In Q. Hassan (Ed.), *Innovative Research and Applications in Next-Generation High Performance Computing* (pp. 349–367). Hershey, PA: IGI Global. doi:10.4018/978-1-5225-0287-6.ch014

Rosado da Cruz, A. M., & Paiva, S. (2016). Cloud and Mobile: A Future Together. In A. Rosado da Cruz & S. Paiva (Eds.), *Modern Software Engineering Methodologies for Mobile and Cloud Environments* (pp. 1–20). Hershey, PA: IGI Global. doi:10.4018/978-1-4666-9916-8.ch001

Rusko, R. (2017). Strategic Turning Points in ICT Business: The Business Development, Transformation, and Evolution in the Case of Nokia. In I. Oncioiu (Ed.), *Driving Innovation and Business Success in the Digital Economy* (pp. 1–15). Hershey, PA: IGI Global. doi:10.4018/978-1-5225-1779-5.ch001

Sahlin, J. P. (2015). Federal Government Application of the Cloud Computing Application Integration Model. In M. Khosrow-Pour (Ed.), *Encyclopedia of Information Science and Technology* (3rd ed.; pp. 2735–2744). Hershey, PA: IGI Global. doi:10.4018/978-1-4666-5888-2.ch267

Sahoo, S., Sahoo, B., Turuk, A. K., & Mishra, S. K. (2017). Real Time Task Execution in Cloud Using MapReduce Framework. In A. Turuk, B. Sahoo, & S. Addya (Eds.), *Resource Management and Efficiency in Cloud Computing Environments* (pp. 190–209). Hershey, PA: IGI Global. doi:10.4018/978-1-5225-1721-4.ch008

Schnjakin, M., & Meinel, C. (2014). Solving Security and Availability Challenges in Public Clouds. In A. Kayem & C. Meinel (Eds.), *Information Security in Diverse Computing Environments* (pp. 280–302). Hershey, PA: IGI Global. doi:10.4018/978-1-4666-6158-5.ch015

Shaikh, F. (2017). The Benefits of New Online (Digital) Technologies on Business: Understanding the Impact of Digital on Different Aspects of the Business. In I. Hosu & I. Iancu (Eds.), *Digital Entrepreneurship and Global Innovation* (pp. 1–17). Hershey, PA: IGI Global. doi:10.4018/978-1-5225-0953-0.ch001

Shalan, M. (2017). Cloud Service Footprint (CSF): Utilizing Risk and Governance Directions to Characterize a Cloud Service. In A. Turuk, B. Sahoo, & S. Addya (Eds.), *Resource Management and Efficiency in Cloud Computing Environments* (pp. 61–88). Hershey, PA: IGI Global. doi:10.4018/978-1-5225-1721-4.ch003

Sharma, A., & Tandekar, P. (2017). Cyber Security and Business Growth. In Rajagopal, & R. Behl (Eds.), Business Analytics and Cyber Security Management in Organizations (pp. 14-27). Hershey, PA: IGI Global. doi:10.4018/978-1-5225-0902-8.ch002

Shen, Y., Li, Y., Wu, L., Liu, S., & Wen, Q. (2014). Big Data Techniques, Tools, and Applications. In Y. Shen, Y. Li, L. Wu, S. Liu, & Q. Wen (Eds.), *Enabling the New Era of Cloud Computing: Data Security, Transfer, and Management* (pp. 185–212). Hershey, PA: IGI Global. doi:10.4018/978-1-4666-4801-2.ch009

Shen, Y., Li, Y., Wu, L., Liu, S., & Wen, Q. (2014). Cloud Infrastructure: Virtualization. In Y. Shen, Y. Li, L. Wu, S. Liu, & Q. Wen (Eds.), *Enabling the New Era of Cloud Computing: Data Security, Transfer, and Management* (pp. 51–76). Hershey, PA: IGI Global. doi:10.4018/978-1-4666-4801-2.ch003

Siddesh, G. M., Srinivasa, K. G., & Tejaswini, L. (2015). Recent Trends in Cloud Computing Security Issues and Their Mitigation. In G. Deka & S. Bakshi (Eds.), *Handbook of Research on Securing Cloud-Based Databases with Biometric Applications* (pp. 16–46). Hershey, PA: IGI Global. doi:10.4018/978-1-4666-6559-0.ch002

Singh, J., Gimekar, A. M., & Venkatesan, S. (2017). An Overview of Big Data Security with Hadoop Framework. In M. Kumar (Ed.), *Applied Big Data Analytics in Operations Management* (pp. 165–181). Hershey, PA: IGI Global. doi:10.4018/978-1-5225-0886-1.ch008

Singh, S., & Singh, J. (2017). Management of SME's Semi Structured Data Using Semantic Technique. In M. Kumar (Ed.), *Applied Big Data Analytics in Operations Management* (pp. 133–164). Hershey, PA: IGI Global. doi:10.4018/978-1-5225-0886-1.ch007

Sokolowski, L., & Oussena, S. (2016). Using Big Data in Collaborative Learning. In M. Atzmueller, S. Oussena, & T. Roth-Berghofer (Eds.), *Enterprise Big Data Engineering, Analytics, and Management* (pp. 221–237). Hershey, PA: IGI Global. doi:10.4018/978-1-5225-0293-7.ch013

Soliman, F. (2015). Evaluation of Cloud System Success Factors in Supply-Demand Chains. In F. Soliman (Ed.), *Business Transformation and Sustainability through Cloud System Implementation* (pp. 90–104). Hershey, PA: IGI Global. doi:10.4018/978-1-4666-6445-6.ch007

Srinivasan, S. (2014). Meeting Compliance Requirements while using Cloud Services. In S. Srinivasan (Ed.), *Security, Trust, and Regulatory Aspects of Cloud Computing in Business Environments* (pp. 127–144). Hershey, PA: IGI Global. doi:10.4018/978-1-4666-5788-5.ch007

Sun, X., & Wei, Z. (2015). The Dynamic Data Privacy Protection Strategy Based on the CAP Theory. *International Journal of Interdisciplinary Telecommunications and Networking*, 7(1), 44–56. doi:10.4018/ijitn.2015010104

Sundararajan, S., Bhasi, M., & Pramod, K. (2017). Managing Software Risks in Maintenance Projects, from a Vendor Perspective: A Case Study in Global Software Development. *International Journal of Information Technology Project Management*, 8(1), 35–54. doi:10.4018/IJITPM.2017010103

Sundaresan, M., & Boopathy, D. (2014). Different Perspectives of Cloud Security. In S. Srinivasan (Ed.), *Security, Trust, and Regulatory Aspects of Cloud Computing in Business Environments* (pp. 73–90). Hershey, PA: IGI Global. doi:10.4018/978-1-4666-5788-5.ch004

Sutagundar, A. V., & Hatti, D. (2017). Data Management in Internet of Things. In N. Kamila (Ed.), *Handbook of Research on Wireless Sensor Network Trends, Technologies, and Applications* (pp. 80–97). Hershey, PA: IGI Global. doi:10.4018/978-1-5225-0501-3.ch004

Swacha, J. (2014). Measuring and Managing the Economics of Information Storage. In T. Tsiakis, T. Kargidis, & P. Katsaros (Eds.), *Approaches and Processes for Managing the Economics of Information Systems* (pp. 47–65). Hershey, PA: IGI Global. doi:10.4018/978-1-4666-4983-5.ch003

Swarnkar, M., & Bhadoria, R. S. (2016). Security Aspects in Utility Computing. In G. Deka, G. Siddesh, K. Srinivasa, & L. Patnaik (Eds.), *Emerging Research Surrounding Power Consumption and Performance Issues in Utility Computing* (pp. 262–275). Hershey, PA: IGI Global. doi:10.4018/978-1-4666-8853-7.ch012

Talamantes-Padilla, C. A., García-Alcaráz, J. L., Maldonado-Macías, A. A., Alor-Hernández, G., Sánchéz-Ramírez, C., & Hernández-Arellano, J. L. (2017). Information and Communication Technology Impact on Supply Chain Integration, Flexibility, and Performance. In M. Tavana, K. Szabat, & K. Puranam (Eds.), *Organizational Productivity and Performance Measurements Using Predictive Modeling and Analytics* (pp. 213–234). Hershey, PA: IGI Global. doi:10.4018/978-1-5225-0654-6.ch011

Tang, Z., & Pan, Y. (2015). Big Data Security Management. In N. Zaman, M. Seliaman, M. Hassan, & F. Marquez (Eds.), *Handbook of Research on Trends and Future Directions in Big Data and Web Intelligence* (pp. 53–66). Hershey, PA: IGI Global. doi:10.4018/978-1-4666-8505-5.ch003

Thakur, P. K., & Verma, A. (2015). Process Batch Offloading Method for Mobile-Cloud Computing Platform. *Journal of Cases on Information Technology*, *17*(3), 1–13. doi:10.4018/JCIT.2015070101

Thota, C., Manogaran, G., Lopez, D., & Vijayakumar, V. (2017). Big Data Security Framework for Distributed Cloud Data Centers. In M. Moore (Ed.), *Cybersecurity Breaches and Issues Surrounding Online Threat Protection* (pp. 288–310). Hershey, PA: IGI Global. doi:10.4018/978-1-5225-1941-6.ch012

Toor, G. S., & Ma, M. (2017). Security Issues of Communication Networks in Smart Grid. In M. Ferrag & A. Ahmim (Eds.), *Security Solutions and Applied Cryptography in Smart Grid Communications* (pp. 29–49). Hershey, PA: IGI Global. doi:10.4018/978-1-5225-1829-7.ch002

Wahi, A. K., Medury, Y., & Misra, R. K. (2015). Big Data: Enabler or Challenge for Enterprise 2.0. *International Journal of Service Science, Management, Engineering, and Technology, 6*(2), 1–17. doi:10.4018/ijssmet.2015040101

Wang, H., Liu, W., & Soyata, T. (2014). Accessing Big Data in the Cloud Using Mobile Devices. In P. Raj & G. Deka (Eds.), *Handbook of Research on Cloud Infrastructures for Big Data Analytics* (pp. 444–470). Hershey, PA: IGI Global. doi:10.4018/978-1-4666-5864-6.ch018

Wang, M., & Kerr, D. (2017). Confidential Data Storage Systems for Wearable Platforms. In A. Marrington, D. Kerr, & J. Gammack (Eds.), *Managing Security Issues and the Hidden Dangers of Wearable Technologies* (pp. 74–97). Hershey, PA: IGI Global. doi:10.4018/978-1-5225-1016-1.ch004

Winter, J. S. (2015). Privacy Challenges for the Internet of Things. In M. Khosrow-Pour (Ed.), *Encyclopedia of Information Science and Technology* (3rd ed.; pp. 4373–4383). Hershey, PA: IGI Global. doi:10.4018/978-1-4666-5888-2.ch429

Wolfe, M. (2017). Establishing Governance for Hybrid Cloud and the Internet of Things. In J. Chen, Y. Zhang, & R. Gottschalk (Eds.), *Handbook of Research on End-to-End Cloud Computing Architecture Design* (pp. 300–325). Hershey, PA: IGI Global. doi:10.4018/978-1-5225-0759-8.ch013

Yan, Z. (2014). Trust Management in Mobile Cloud Computing. In *Trust Management in Mobile Environments: Autonomic and Usable Models* (pp. 54–93). Hershey, PA: IGI Global. doi:10.4018/978-1-4666-4765-7.ch004

Zardari, M. A., & Jung, L. T. (2016). Classification of File Data Based on Confidentiality in Cloud Computing using K-NN Classifier. *International Journal of Business Analytics, 3*(2), 61–78. doi:10.4018/IJBAN.2016040104

Related Readings

Zhang, C., Simon, J. C., & Lee, E. (2016). An Empirical Investigation of Decision Making in IT-Related Dilemmas: Impact of Positive and Negative Consequence Information. *Journal of Organizational and End User Computing*, *28*(4), 73–90. doi:10.4018/JOEUC.2016100105

Zou, J., Wang, Y., & Orgun, M. A. (2015). Modeling Accountable Cloud Services Based on Dynamic Logic for Accountability. *International Journal of Web Services Research*, *12*(3), 48–77. doi:10.4018/IJWSR.2015070103

Compilation of References

Augur. (2016). *Augur: Reference Client*. Retrieved from http://docs.augur. net/#overview

Back, A. (2002). *Hashcash-a denial of service counter-measure*. Academic Press.

Beck, M. (2010). *Centralized versus Decentralized Information Systems in Organizations*. Emporia State University.

Biella, M. (2016). *Blockchain Technology and Applications from a Financial Perspective: Technical Report, Data & Analytics*. Coindesk.

Bitcoin Foundation Wiki. (2016). *Blockchain*. Retrieved from https:// en.bitcoin.it/wiki/Block_chain

Bitcoin.org. (2009). *Bitcoin Developer Guide*. Retrieved from https://bitcoin. org/en/developer-guide

Bitnation. (2016). *Public Notary System: Bitnation*. Retrieved from https:// bitnation.co/notary/

Bogdan, D. (2016). *Decentralised social media: doing it the blockchain way*. Retrieved from http://www.coinfox.info/news/reviews/5846-blockchain-social-media

Buterin, V. (2013a). *Ethereum white paper*. Ethereum.

Buterin, V. (2013b). *What Proof of Stake is and Why it Matters*. bitcoin-magazine.com.

Buterin, V. (2014). *A next-generation smart contract and decentralized application platform*. White Paper.

Castillo, M. (2016). *Nasdaq Opens Blockchain Services to Global Exchange Partners*. Retrieved from http://www.coindesk.com/nasdaqs-blockchain-services-global-exchange/

Chaum, D. (1984). Blind signature system. In Advances in cryptology (pp. 153-153). Springer US. doi:10.1007/978-1-4684-4730-9_14

Christoph. (2016). *Mist*. Retrieved from https://daowiki.atlassian.net/wiki/display/DAO/Mist

Click, R., Shutzberg, L., & Buren, M. V. (2006). *Centralized vs. Distributed Computing: How to Decide*. ExecBlueprints.

Corridori, A. F. (2012). *What is Centralized Computing*. Retrieved July 5, 2016 from http://idcp.marist.edu/enterprisesystemseducation/zinsights/ECI%20No.%202%20Cent%20Comp%20v2c.pdf

Crosby, M., Nachippan, Pattanayak P., Verma S., & Kalyanaraman, V. (2015). *BlockChain Technology Beyond Bitcoin*. Sutardja Center for Entrepreneurship & Technology Technical Report.

Crosby, M., Pattanayak, P., Verma, S., & Kalyanaraman, V. (2016). Blockchain technology: Beyond bitcoin. *Applied Innovation*, (2), 6-10.

Delmolino, K., Arnett, M., Kosba, A., Miller, A., & Shi, E. (2015). *A programmer's guide to ethereum and serpent*. Retrieved from:https://mc2-umd.github.io/ethereumlab/docs/serpent_tutorial.pdf

DTCC. (2016). *Embracing Disruption: Tapping The Potential Of Distributed Ledgers To Improve The Post-Trade Landscape*. Retrieved from https://www.finextra.com/finextra-downloads/newsdocs/embracing%20disruption%20white%20paper_final_jan-16.pdf

Ethdocs. (2016). *The Ethereum Network*. Retrieved from http://ethdocs.org/en/latest/network/index.html

Ethereum Builder's Guide. (2016). *Serpent Features*. Retrieved from https://ethereumbuilders.gitbooks.io/guide/content/en/serpent_features.html

Ethereum Homestead Documentation. (2016). Retrieved from http://ethdocs.org/en/latest/

Higgins, S. (2016). *LHV Bank Develops Wallet App Built on Bitcoin's Blockchain*. Retrieved from http://www.coindesk.com/lhv-bank-backs-wallet-app-built-on-bitcoins-blockchain/

Hudson. (2016). *Creating a Private Chain/Testnet*. Retrieved from https://souptacular.gitbooks.io/ethereum-tutorials-and-tips-by-hudson/content/private-chain.html

Hyperledger. (2016). *Blockchain rewires financial markets: Trailblazers take the lead*. IBM Institute for Business Value.

IBM Blockchain. (2016). *The Hyperledger Project*. Retrieved from http://www.ibm.com/blockchain/hyperledger.html

IBM. (2016). *Walmart, IBM and Tsinghua University Explore the Use of Blockchain to Help Bring Safer Food to Dinner Tables Across China*. Retrieved from https://www-03.ibm.com/press/us/en/pressrelease/50816.wss

Iurimatias. (2016). *Embark Framework*. Retrieved from https://github.com/iurimatias/embark-framework/blob/develop/README.md

Jakobsson, M., & Juels, A. (1999). Proofs of work and bread pudding protocols. In Secure Information Networks (pp. 258-272). Springer US.

Johnsen, J. A., Karlsen, L. E., & Birkeland, S. S. (2005). *Peer-to-peer networking with BitTorrent*. Department of Telematics, NTNU.

Kakavand, H., & Kost De Sevres, N. (2016). *The Blockchain Revolution: An Analysis of Regulation and Technology Related to Distributed Ledger Technologies*. Academic Press.

Kapplerken. (2016). *Your first Dapp*. Retrieved from https://dappsforbeginners.wordpress.com/tutorials/your-first-dapp/

Kastelein, R. (2016). *Everledger Rolls Out Blockchain Technology to Digitally Certify Kimberley Diamonds*. Retrieved from http://www.the-blockchain.com/2016/09/20/everledger-rolls-out-blockchain-technology-to-digitally-certify-kimberley-diamonds/

Kate. (2016). *Blockchain Will Define the Future of Social Networks*. Retrieved from https://letstalkpayments.com/blockchain-will-define-the-future-of-social-networks/

King, J. L. (1983). Centralized versus decentralized computing: Organizational considerations and management options. *ACM Computing Surveys, 15*(4), 319–349. doi:10.1145/289.290

Kralingen, B. (2016). *How Blockchain Could Help To Make The Food We Eat Safer... Around The World.* IBM. Retrieved from http://www.forbes.com/sites/ibm/2016/11/01/how-blockchain-could-help-to-make-the-food-we-eat-safer-around-the-world/#41fbbe3d67df

Lazooz. (2016). *Lazooz: White Paper.* Retrieved from http://lazooz.org/whitepaper.html

Lewis, A. (2015). A gentle introduction to blockchain technology. *Bits on Blocks.* Retrieved from https://bitsonblocks.net/2015/09/09/a-gentle-introduction-to-blockchain-technology/

LTP. (2016). *Know more about blockchain: Overview, technology, application areas and use cases.* Retrieved from https://letstalkpayments.com/an-overview-of-blockchain-technology/

Luu, L., Chu, D. H., Olickel, H., Saxena, P., & Hobor, A. (2016, October). Making smart contracts smarter. In *Proceedings of the 2016 ACM SIGSAC Conference on Computer and Communications Security* (pp. 254-269). ACM. doi:10.1145/2976749.2978309

Mattila, J. (2016). *The Blockchain Phenomenon–The Disruptive Potential of Distributed Consensus Architectures (No. 38).* The Research Institute of the Finnish Economy.

Mist. (2016). *Mist Browser.* Retrieved from https://github.com/ethereum/mist

Mougayar, W. (2015). *Understanding the blockchain.* Retrieved from https://www.oreilly.com/ideas/understanding-the-blockchain

MSG. (2016). *Centralization and Decentralization.* Retrieved from http://www.managementstudyguide.com/centralization_decentralization.htm

Nakamoto, S. (2008). *Bitcoin: A peer-to-peer electronic cash system.* Academic Press.

O'Dair, M., Beaven, Z., Neilson, D., Osborne, R., & Pacifico, P. (2016). *Music on the blockchain.* Academic Press.

Panikkar, S., Nair, S., Brody, P., & Pureswaran, V. (2014). *ADEPT: An IoT Practitioner Perspective*. IBM Institute for Business Value.

Pilkington, M. (2016). *Blockchain technology: principles and applications. In Research Handbook on Digital Transformations*. Edward Elgar.

Price, R. (2016). *Bitcoin Mining*. Retrieved from https://www.doc.ic.ac.uk/project/2015/163/g1516329/website/Proof-of-Work/proof_of_work.html

Prisco, G. (2016a). *MIT Media Lab Releases Code for Digital Certificates on the Blockchain*. Retrieved from https://bitcoinmagazine.com/articles/mit-media-lab-releases-code-for-digital-certificates-on-the-blockchain-1465404945

Prisco, G. (2016a). *Santander Becomes First U.K. Bank to Introduce Blockchain Technology for International Payments*. Retrieved from https://bitcoinmagazine.com/articles/santander-becomes-first-u-k-bank-to-introduce-blockchain-technology-for-international-payments-1464795902

Prisco, G. (2016b). *Bitnation Launches World's First Blockchain-Based Virtual Nation Constitution*. Retrieved from https://bitcoinmagazine.com/articles/bitnation-launches-world-s-first-blockchain-based-virtual-nation-constitution-1455895473

Prisco, G. (2016b). *Slock.it to Introduce Smart Locks Linked to Smart Ethereum Contracts, Decentralize the Sharing Economy*. Retrieved from https://bitcoinmagazine.com/articles/slock-it-to-introduce-smart-locks-linked-to-smart-ethereum-contracts-decentralize-the-sharing-economy-1446746719

Pureswaran, V., Panikkar, S., Nair, S., & Brody, P. (2015). *Empowering the edge: Practical insights on a decentralized Internet of Things*. IBM Institute for Business Value.

Redman, J. (2015). *Neureal: Bringing Artificial Intelligence to the People*. Retrieved from https://cointelegraph.com/news/neureal-bringing-artificial-intelligence-to-the-people

Remix. (2016). Retrieved from https://github.com/ethereum/remix

Rosenfeld, M. (2012). *Overview of colored coins*. White paper, bitcoil. co. il.

Sfertman. (2016). *Mix: The DApp IDE*. Retrieved from https://github.com/ethereum/wiki/wiki/Mix:-The-DApp-IDE

Shieber, J. (2015). *Microsoft Partners With ConsenSys To Use Ethereum To Provide Blockchain-As-A-Service*. Retrieved from https://techcrunch.com/2015/10/28/microsoft-partners-with-consensys-to-use-ethereum-to-provide-blockchain-as-a-service/

Sofia. (2016). *Blockchain-Enabled Smart Contracts: Applications and Challenges*. Retrieved from https://letstalkpayments.com/blockchain-enabled-smart-contracts-applications-and-challenges/

Solidity Tutorials. (2016). Retrieved from https://ethereumbuilders.gitbooks.io/guide/content/en/solidity_tutorials.html

Solidity. (2016). Retrieved from https://solidity.readthedocs.io/en/develop/

Stratumn. (2016). *Stratumn and Deloitte unveil blockchain-based micro-insurance PoC*. Retrieved from https://www.finextra.com/pressarticle/65264/stratumn-and-deloitte-unveil-blockchain-based-micro-insurance-poc

Suryanarayana, G. (2006). *Decentralization: PACE Project*. Retrieved from http://isr.uci.edu/projects/pace/decentralization.html

Swan, M. (2015). Blockchain thinking: The brain as a dac (decentralized autonomous organization).*Texas Bitcoin Conference*.

Swan, M. (2015). *Blockchain: Blueprint for a new economy*. O'Reilly Media, Inc.

Szabo, N. (1997). *The idea of smart contracts*. Nick Szabo's Papers and Concise Tutorials.

Tapscott, D., & Tapscott, A. (2016). *How Blockchain Technology Can Reinvent The Power Grid*. Retrieved from http://fortune.com/2016/05/15/blockchain-reinvents-power-grid/

Tatowicz, A. (2016). *Dapp using Meteor*. Retrieved from https://github.com/ethereum/wiki/wiki/Dapp-using-Meteor

The Next Galaxy. (2016). *The Advantages and Disadvantages of Decentralization*. Retrieved from http://thenextgalaxy.com/the-advantages-and-disadvantages-of-decentralization/

Tieron. (2016). *Blockchain Healthcare 2016 Report – Promise & Pitfalls*. Retrieved from https://tierion.com/blog/blockchain-healthcare-2016-report/

Toole, R., & Vokkarane, V. (2006). *Bittorrent architecture and protocol.* University of Massachusetts Dartmouth.

Truffle. (2016). Retrieved from http://truffle.readthedocs.io/en/latest/

Wagner, A. (2016). *Smart Property in Action.* Retrieved from https://bitcoin-magazine.com/articles/smart-property-action-1408049337

Wall Street Journal. (2014). *The Imminent Decentralized Computing Revolution.* Retrieved from http://blogs.wsj.com/accelerators/2014/10/10/weekend-read-the-imminent-decentralized-computing-revolution/

Walport, M. (2016). Distributed Ledger Technology: Beyond Blockchain. UK Government Office for Science, Tech. Rep, 19.

Wilkinson, S., Lowry, J., & Boshevski, T. (2014). *Metadisk a blockchain-based decentralized file storage application.* Technical Report. Retrieved from http://metadisk. org/metadisk.pdf

Wood, G. (2014). *Ethereum Yellow Paper.* Ethereum.

About the Authors

S. Asharaf is an Associate Professor at Indian Institute of Information Technology and Management – Kerala. He is also serving as a visiting faculty in Indian Institute of Space Science and Technology, Trivandrum and as a Mentor in Kerala Startup Mission. He received his PhD and Master of Engineering degrees in Computer Science from Indian Institute of Science, Bangalore. He graduated in Computer Engineering from Cochin University of Science and Technology. After his PhD he has worked with America Online (AOL) and IIM Kozhikode. He is a recipient of IBM outstanding PhD student award 2006 and IBM Shared University Research Grant, 2015. He has published two books and more than 25 research papers in international journals and conferences. His areas of interest include technologies and business models related to machine learning, information retrieval, web mining and intelligent internet of things. Web Link: https://in.linkedin.com/in/asharafs.

S. Adarsh is a Research Scholar at Indian Institute of Information Technology and Management – Kerala, doing research under the guidance of Dr. Asharaf S. He is a recipient of Junior Research Fellowship in Engineering Sciences, 2014 from Kerala State Council for Science, Technology & Environment (KSCSTE). He did Masters and Bachelor of Engineering degrees at TKM Institute of Technology, Kollam under the Cochin University of Science and Technology. After doing his Masters he worked as Assistant Professor at Sree Buddha College of Engineering under the Kerala University. His areas of interest include blockchains and smart contracts, machine learning and bio-inspired computing. Web Link: https://in.linkedin.com/in/adarsh-s-28a195113.

Index

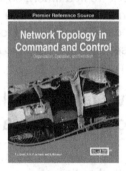

Support Your Colleagues and Stay Current on the Latest Research Developments

Become a Reviewer

In this competitive age of scholarly publishing, constructive and timely feedback significantly decreases the turn-around time of manuscripts from submission to acceptance, allowing the publication and discovery of progressive research at a much more expeditious rate.

The overall success of a refereed journal is dependent on quality and timely reviews.

Several IGI Global journals are currently seeking highly qualified experts in the field to fill vacancies on their respective editorial review boards. Reviewing manuscripts allows you to stay current on the latest developments in your field of research, while at the same time providing constructive feedback to your peers.

Reviewers are expected to write reviews in a timely, collegial, and constructive manner. All reviewers will begin their role on an ad-hoc basis for a period of one year, and upon successful completion of this term can be considered for full editorial review board status, with the potential for a subsequent promotion to Associate Editor.

Join this elite group by visiting the IGI Global journal webpage, and clicking on "**Become a Reviewer**".

Applications may also be submitted online at:
www.igi-global.com/journals/become-a-reviewer/.

Applicants must have a doctorate (or an equivalent degree) as well as publishing and reviewing experience.

If you have a colleague that may be interested in this opportunity, we encourage you to share this information with them.

Any questions regarding this opportunity can be sent to:
journaleditor@igi-global.com.

Printed in the United States
By Bookmasters